Library of
Davidson College

I, MARK: a personal encounter

a personal

I, MARK
encounter

*Explorations
in the earliest Gospel*

CARL WALTERS, Jr.

John Knox Press
ATLANTA

Unless otherwise indicated Scripture quotations are from the Revised Standard Version of the Holy Bible, copyright, 1946, 1952, and © 1971, 1973 by the Division of Christian Education, National Council of the Churches of Christ in the U.S.A. and used by permission.

Library of Congress Cataloging in Publication Data
Walters, Carl F. 1934—
  I, Mark.

  Includes index.
  1. Bible. N.T. Mark—Criticism, interpretation, etc. I. Title.
BS2585.2.W34   226'.3'06   78-52450
ISBN 0-8042-0272-9 pbk.

© copyright 1980 John Knox Press
10 9 8 7 6 5 4 3 2 1

Printed in the United States of America
Atlanta, Georgia 30308

To Robin

acknowledgments

I want to express here, simply and sincerely, my deep and abiding gratitude to my past teachers: particularly Professors John Bright, Balmer Kelly, Howard MacRae, James Mays, and Donald Miller, who both instructed and inspired me in the disciplines of biblical languages, history, literature, and interpretation at Union Theological Seminary, Richmond, Virginia; and my present teachers: those other scholar-mentors whom I do not know personally, but to whom, through their works, I am enormously indebted. I am also grateful to my students, past and present, whose contributions and questions in New Testament courses have effectively prompted me to further inquiry. They have also challenged me to seek new and appropriate ways of apprehending and communicating the original meanings of the early Christian documents, in this case, specifically, the Gospel of Mark. Although there is little which might be called original in this exploration, those professional tutors and colleagues, upon whom I am so dependent, should in nowise be held responsible for any inadequacies which may be discovered. Undoubtedly these are my own.

Further, I wish to express my appreciation to President James H. Daughdrill, Jr., of Southwestern At Memphis, for facilitating initial communication with John Knox Press and encouraging me in the writing of this my first book. Probably without this assistance and support I would not have undertaken this writing at this time. It is certain that this book could not have come to completion without the continuing encouragement, the patient guidance, and the helpful suggestions of Dr. Richard Ray, Director and Editor, and Mr. R. Donald Hardy, Associate Editor, of John Knox Press. To them and their staff, especially, Joan Crawford, whose perceptive and careful work really brought this book into its final, readable form, I offer my hearty and unreserved thanks. My grateful appreciation is also gladly expressed to Harriett Hardy who read the manuscript as it neared completion and offered not only positive reinforcements but also constructive criticisms and insightful suggestions for improvements. To my sister, Judy Walters Ritter, who graciously consented to read the manuscript in its entirety and who offered invaluable editorial assistance, I am deeply indebted and thankful.

To Ms. Candis Young, our 1977-78 student secretary in the department of religion, who typed and retyped the manuscript, who encouraged me with positive comments, and who also further assisted me with pertinent critiques from the youthful student's perspective, I am especially grateful. I am grateful also to Ms. Dee Strock, my 1978-79 student secretarial assistant, for her help in the retyping of the manuscript, proofreading and preparation of the "Index to References in Mark." In this last tedious task Ms. Strock was ably assisted by another student, Ms. Lydia Haff.

My family (wife Robin, son Jeffrey, and daughter Lucy) have graciously tolerated this literary preoccupation; my mental, if not physical, absence; and my preemptory and presumptive occupation of our breakfast room and its table, which has been cluttered with books and papers for all these months. Words cannot express my thankfulness to them for their understanding, patience, and supportive love. Individually and corporately they personify one of the main motifs of Mark: in the face of all nos the divine definitive word is yes; through all difficulties, distresses, and deaths, for the people of faith, the present experience and the final fact is liberated life!

The section "Christ and Conflict: An Essay on a Theme" and the fourteen "interpretive reflections" on selected passages from Mark originated as an introductory article and brief weekly commentaries for teachers of adults in the *U.L.C.S. Teacher (Uniform Lessons Cooperative Series: International Bible Lessons for Christian Teaching),* January-March, 1969. Although these remain much the same as in their original publication, they have been considerably supplemented, revised and rewritten in numerous places. Grateful acknowledgment is hereby made to *U.L.C.S. Teacher* for permission to use this material in its present form.

contents

Some Suggestions for Reading and Using This Book   10

PART I: METHODOLOGY   12

Yesterday and Today   14

The Present Gratefully Indebted to the Past: Scholarly Approaches Which Have Informed This Study of Mark   15
- Literary Criticism   15
- Form Criticism   15
- Redaction Criticism   20
- Structural Exegesis   21

ANAWATUK IN THE ORANGE GROVE: A Parable about Bible Study   23

PART II: ST. MARK SPEAKS   26

A Short Explanatory Note from the Author   26

The Setting for St. Mark's Address   28

ST. MARK'S ADDRESS   28
- Many Saints   28
- Many "Authors"   29
- Anonymity   30
- The Traditional Mark   30
- The Real Mark Stands Up   32
- An Unfinished Drama That Continues   33
- The Main Subject and Four Preliminary Remarks   34
- Soteriology (Suffering and Salvation)   38
- Christology (Titles for Jesus)   49
- Eschatology (Final Fulfillment)   57
- Theological Editorial Techniques   61
- Outlines   70

PART III: ST. MARK HEARD 74

CHRIST AND CONFLICT: An Essay on a Theme 76

    Conflict in the Cosmos 77
    Conflict in Palestine 81
    Conflict in Rome 88
    Conflict in Contemporary Culture 96

INTERPRETIVE REFLECTIONS ON REPRESENTATIVE PASSAGES IN MARK'S GOSPEL 98

    The Beginning of the Good News (Mark 1:1–20) 98
    Jesus' Teaching: Exorcising Demons, Healing Diseases, and Preaching the Gospel (Mark 1:21–45) 105
    Early Reactions to Jesus (Mark 2:1—3:6) 107
    People Misunderstand Jesus—Demons Do Not! (Mark 3:7–35) 110
    Teachings about the Kingdom (Mark 4:1–34) 113
    The Mighty Power of Jesus (Mark 4:35—6:6) 115
    Disciples Called and Commissioned (Mark 6:7–56) 118
    When Religion Is Vital It Is Not Exclusive (Mark 7:1—8:26) 120
    The Christ Must Suffer—His Disciples Must Follow (Mark 8:27–37) 122
    Poverty and Riches: The Meaning of Discipleship (Mark 10) 125
    The Authority of Jesus (Mark 11—12) 127
    A Symbolic Supper and a Time of Testing (Mark 14:22–26, 32–42) 129
    Jesus Rejected and Crucified (Mark 14:53–65; 15:16–39) 132
    He Has Risen! (Mark 15:42—16:8) 134

Notes 136

Index to References in Mark 143

some suggestions for reading and using this book

1. Obviously, this book can be read and studied straight through, from start to finish. The rationale for its order is indicated in the titles of the three main parts: "Part I: Methodology" (both in the writing and the reading of this book), "Part II: St. Mark Speaks," "Part III: St. Mark Heard." Part I is an explanation and an introduction to the plan and procedure of this book. It includes some illustrations of scholarly approaches to the Synoptic Gospels of the New Testament (Matthew, Mark, and Luke) which have informed this study of the Gospel According to Mark. It concludes with the story of Anawatuk, a short "parabolic" prologue suggesting, in fable-fashion, three ways which are inappropriate, and one way which is appropriate for approaching and interpreting biblical documents. Part II is an application of the interpretive methods (especially redaction criticism) explained in Part I. Part III consists of an essay on a dominant Markan theme and interpretations of fourteen representative sections from Mark's Gospel.

2. If "Part II: St. Mark Speaks" feels a little too unfamiliar, advanced, or detailed, it might be a good idea to go directly from "Part I: Methodology," to Part III: St. Mark Heard" (the essay "Christ and Conflict" and the fourteen "interpretive reflections"). After that the reader could come back to "Part II: St. Mark Speaks," and read on through the sections it contains. The themes of these sections surface again in several places in the interpretive reflections (Part III). The meanings which are suggested in the interpretive reflections are previewed in the thematic and editorial analysis given in Mark's "address." The numerous cross-references in Parts II and III of this book indicate their interrelatedness. The two parts *are* dialogical. Part II is intended to be the opening statement in the conversation or, to use another metaphor, the recipe (the ingredients and the baking procedure) for the pie which is to be sliced and eaten in Part III.

3. Have a Bible at hand and use it. (The Revised Standard Version, Oxford Annotated edition, is highly recommended.) This book is not intended as a

substitute for reading the Gospel of Mark itself. It was written to be read with constant reference to the biblical text of Mark (and other biblical documents). The contexts in which references are made to the Bible are meant to be interpretive comments.

4. One direct way into the biblical text would be to use the outlines which are given near the end of Mark's address, and following each of them individually, read straight through the Gospel. If each of these is followed that will be about six readings of Mark's Gospel! Remember it's short. And this would be good preparation for an exploration of Mark with the assistance of this guide, following either of the approaches suggested above. Certainly the Gospel of Mark deserves numerous readings and serious study. It is a rich mine full of valuable ore. It will not be depleted by much digging.

5. Make use of the "Index to References in Mark" at the back. By so doing you will find that this book can serve as a brief and introductory commentary on numerous texts and passages in the Gospel of Mark. This is in addition to the fourteen interpretive reflections on representative passages ("Part III: St. Mark Heard").

PART I:

Methodology

Informed and responsible study of the Bible today presupposes a basic awareness and a working knowledge of the essential data and the appropriate techniques which have been gathered and developed within this discipline over many generations. The purpose of this first section on "methodology" is to provide the reader with this basic awareness and working knowledge pertaining particularly to the Gospel of Mark. Therefore, the procedure of Part I is four-fold: (1) To present a brief, simplified, and historical sketch of New Testament Gospel research in the modern period (roughly the nineteenth and twentieth centuries) focusing mainly on methods of literary analysis. (2) To describe and illustrate those literary interpretive methods which have been developed in the past and are employed in the present. (3) To indicate how these methods are used and reflected in *this* study of the Gospel of Mark and to invite the reader to experience their application and results firsthand in Parts II and III. (4) To inform the reader of the plan and procedure of this book and thereby, to lead the reader into its most effective and enjoyable use.

Yesterday and Today

Biblical scholarship is an accumulative discipline. Each generation of interpreters learns from, builds upon, seeks to correct, and attempts to go beyond those who have gone before. It is necessary to understand something of the past in order to participate, with awareness and effectiveness, in what is happening in the present. Informed and responsible students of the New Testament today use interpretive tools and employ interpretive methods which were developed by their predecessors.

In order to understand the meanings of ancient documents for modern life, as adequately and accurately as possible, we must learn as much as we can about the historico-cultural contexts in which they were written. That includes the life-situations, attitudes, and interests of their authors; the meanings of the words and the dynamics of the languages in which they were written; and the processes, oral and/or literary, by which they were produced.

Contemporary interpreters of the New Testament Gospels are the heirs of their scholarly forebears in all these matters. They are the beneficiaries of the accumulated wealth, the knowledge and skills of those who have preceded them. Much of the information gathered in the past they have retained unchanged; much of it they have corrected or modified or supplemented; some of it they have rejected, having tested it and found it either inaccurate or misleading, or both. Needless to say there has *never* been unanimous agreement among scholars on all or any of the questions, issues, and decisions involved in this multi-faceted study. However, several of the insightful solutions to primary problems, basic interpretive tools, and fundamental interpretive methods discovered and developed by our predecessors have been found by many current students of the New Testament to be so appropriate, effective, and helpful in discerning and disclosing the original and continuing meanings of the biblical texts that they have simply been retained, sharpened, and used with increasing gratitude.

Generally speaking, the guiding principle which most scholars of the New Testament today are trying to follow is two-fold: (1) to discern as accurately and adequately as possible the cultural, religious, and literary influences upon, the experiences and ideas presupposed by, the meanings written into, and the processes by which the documents were produced; (2) to develop tools and apply methods which are *consistent* with this continually growing body of knowledge.

Now let us familiarize ourselves with the present situation by a quick sketch of the relatively recent past. In the process we will be introduced to methods and become acquainted with basic terms.

The Present Gratefully Indebted to the Past: Scholarly Approaches Which Have Informed This Study of Mark

The present state of our knowledge concerning the most basic and most important questions pertaining to the Gospel of Mark (such as authorship, date, place of composition, sources, structure, purpose, theological themes, and reflected community concerns) is characterized by flux, uncertainty, incompleteness, and variety in scholarly opinion.[1] Indeed, one could have written even an exploratory study on the Gospel of Mark with much more confidence and much less wariness sixty years ago, prior to the rise and development of *Form Criticism,* than one can today. In the meantime *Redaction Criticism* has grown out of *Form Criticism* and the situation has increased in complexity. Currently we are confronted by the challenge of *Structural Exegesis.* Long gone are the simple "good ole days" when one could assume, before or as a result of *Literary Criticism,* that the author of the Gospel of Mark, probably a one-time companion of Paul and a faithful interpreter of Peter (the John Mark of Acts 12:12; 1 Peter 5:13) sat down, as it were, with papyrus and pen in hand and, from oral reports of eyewitnesses, apostolic sermons and lessons, and his own memory wrote the story of Jesus and its meaning from start to finish. Today, using the results of past and present scholarship as torchlights and guide maps we must explore the landscape of this ancient document looking for clues to its structure, purpose, and meaning. Let us now consider briefly some of these aids for our exploration.

Literary Criticism (or *Source Criticism* as it is sometimes called) has its modern roots in the objective (scientific) literary analysis which was brought to bear on all important ancient documents, including the Bible, by humanistic scholars in Europe (mainly Germany and England) during the second half of the eighteenth and the nineteenth centuries. In the area of New Testament study literary criticism sought to account for the many close similarities, as well as the obvious and significant differences, among the Gospels in their content, wording, sequence of events, and arrangement of their material. The most important and continuing result of this 150 plus years of intensive and massive research was the discovery that Mark was the earliest written Gospel, that Matthew and Luke used Mark, plus a "sayings source" (designated "Q" from the German word for source, "Quelle"), and material peculiar to each in the formation of their documents. The Gospel of John was found to be distinctly different from the other three in much of its content and order, its style, and its language.[2]

Form Criticism (or *Formgeschichte,* as the German scholars who initiated this kind of literary analysis called it, meaning the history of the forms) explores back behind the written documents (e.g., the Gospel of Mark) into the previous period of oral transmission of traditions about Jesus. The purpose of *Form Criticism* is to identify the separate units of material within a completed document (for example, parables, pronouncement (saying) stories, miracle stories, etc.) and to attempt to reconstruct how these component parts of the Gospels originated, why they were preserved, how they were shaped and used in the early Christian communities.³ In order to illustrate the relevance of the identification of forms in the interpretation of Mark's Gospel, and in order to portend one of the interpretive methods as well as some of the theological motifs to come, let us reflect briefly upon one of each of the forms named above.

(1) Parable: The Parable of the Vineyard (Mark 12:1–12)

Some scholars maintain that this parable, as it stands in the text *in its present form* (12:1–8 or 1–11) was spoken *verbatim* by Jesus. Many others claim that a nucleus of this story (e.g., vss. 1–5, 9) probably goes back to Jesus himself, but that this nucleus has been added to and shaped by the early church, the community which professes faith in Jesus as the crucified Son of God (vss. 6–8) and the living Lord (vs. 10). Other scholars insist that the entire parable, which appears to be at least partly allegorical (the owner of the vineyard is God, the son is Jesus, the vineyard is Israel, the tenants are the Jewish leaders, and the servants are apparently the Old Testament prophets), was constructed entirely within the Christian community during the period of oral transmission of Gospel material (ca. 30–60 A.D.), placed in the mouth of Jesus and employed in evangelistic preaching and catechetical teaching. The old age is over; the new era has arrived (cf. 1:14–15). Jesus was (is) the suffering, dying, living, reigning Son of God (vss. 6–8, 10–11; cf. 1:11). As such, he is the fulfillment of prophetic prediction (cf. Isa. 5:1–7) and the actualization of poetic vision of (cf. Ps. 118:21–25). Indeed, his rejection by Israel and his subsequent elevation to preeminence were foretold in the scriptures (vss. 10–11; Ps. 118:22–23f.; cf. also 1 Cor. 15:3–4f.).

Regardless of one's conclusion about the origin and history of this parable, as one reads it or hears it within the context of Mark's overall message it is clearly *kerygmatic,* i.e., it is a preachment, pronouncement, or proclamation of the gospel. Furthermore, it is also *didactic,* i.e., it is a lesson, an instruction, an explanation. It teaches that Judaism, the old covenant community of Israel, is no longer the medium of God's saving message, the instrument of God's redemptive action, the locus of God's liberation unto life; rather, the community of the new covenant, the new family of God (brothers and sisters of the Son), the Christian community, the church *is* (vs. 9; cf. 14:22–25; 3:31–35). (See further comments on Jesus' cursing the fig tree [11:12–14, 20] and cleansing the temple [11:15–19]). This sermon/instruction in story form would be immediately and urgently relevant to persons experiencing conflict between Jewish synagogue and Christian church, or Jewish Christians and Gentile Christians *within* the church.

(2) Pronouncement (Saying) Story: "The Things That Are Caesar's and the Things That Are God's (Mark 12:13–17)

The main feature, the most important part of this short story, is the saying of Jesus' which climaxes and concludes it (vs. 17), plus the final note that "they were amazed at him." The setting (vss. 13–16) is subservient to the saying (vs. 17). Form critics disagree among themselves (as above with regard to the parable of the vineyard) on questions such as the authenticity of this saying (did it actually originate with Jesus or was it created first by a Christian or group of believers and attributed to Jesus?), its original historical setting (Jerusalem or elsewhere?), and to what degree it has been fashioned in order to meet the needs of early Christian communities for preaching, teaching, exhortation, etc. Supposing that this pronouncement story with its climactic saying (vs. 17) did originate in the setting described in the text, it is, nevertheless, identifiable now as a memorable and transmittable oral-written form. It includes (1) a setting or incidental context plus (2) a cogent, penetrating, telling word, or pronouncement, as its concluding-climaxing main point (cf. Mark 2:23–28). Regardless of its original setting, in its present form, within the total context of Mark's message, it is a word of both exhortation and encouragement to first-century Christians experiencing conflict between the claims of Caesar and the claims of Christ. (For further interpretive comments on this passage see below.)

(3) Miracle Story: Healing the Man with the Withered Hand (Mark 3:1–6)

The Gospels are full of stories telling about wonderful works of Jesus (exorcisms, e.g., Matt. 8:28–34; Mark 5:1–13; Luke 8:26–39; healings, e.g., Matt. 9:1–8; Mark 2:1–12; Luke 5:17–26; nature miracles, e.g., Matt. 8:18, 23–27; Mark 4:35–41; Luke 8:22–25; raisings from the dead, e.g., Matt. 9:18–26; Mark 5:21–24, 35–43; Luke 8:40–56). Stories about "miracle workers" in the ancient world are not rare. The meaning of the "miracle" and the significance of the "worker" which the story seeks to convey are the important questions or issues.

In oral-literary *form* the normal miracle story consisted of three parts: (1) the setting, including the situation calling for the wonderful act (e.g., a crippled body, a demon possessed person) and the attitude of the one (or ones) upon whom or for whom the deed will be performed (e.g., Mark 1:40; 2:1–5a; 3:1–4; 10:46–51); (2) the action of the wonder-worker, often accompanied by words which affect (and sometimes interpret) the miracle (e.g.,

1:41; 2:5, 11; 5:41); (3) the response, or reaction, of those who witness the wonderful work (e.g., 1:27; 2:12; 3:6; 4:41).

In the story of the healing of the man with the withered hand the setting (3:1–4) is one of conflict or controversy. (Some scholars suggest that this is a combination of two forms, a controversy story and a miracle story). The question is about the proper observance of sabbath law. Legally, healing on the sabbath day was classified by the authorities as work; it was performing the profession of a physician. As such it was a violation of a strict interpretation and application of the fourth commandment (" 'Remember the sabbath day, to keep it holy. Six days you shall labor, and do all your work; but the seventh day is a sabbath [rest] to the LORD your God; in it you shall not do any work. . . .' " Exod. 20:8–10). Jesus, in the synagogue, asks: " 'Is it lawful on the sabbath to do good or to do harm, to save life or to kill?' " By healing the man's hand, saying, " 'Stretch out your hand,' " Jesus breaks the current strict interpretation-application of the divine commandment; but he also goes back and recovers and enacts the original intent of this law: rest, refreshment, restoration of wholeness and life. The Jewish religious leaders and moral teachers (the scribes, Pharisees, lawyers, elders) who had identified the original meaning and intent of the life-giving law with their death-dealing legalism were offended at Jesus. "The Pharisees went out, and immediately held counsel with the Herodians against him, how to destroy him." (3:6; cf. 2:23–28; 7:1–23)

We need not doubt that an actual event of conflict and healing lies behind this story as we now find it in the text of Mark even if we discern its traditional three-part form (3:1–4, 5, 6). At the same time it would not be surprising if, in the preservation, transmission, and employment of this story, first in oral, then in written form within the early church it was shaped in certain ways so that it would speak directly and instructively to the Christian community in controversy with the Jewish synagogue, and to Christian congregations in which there was conflict between Jewish and Gentile believers over serious matters of law-keeping, such as sabbath observance (3:1–2; cf. 2:23–28). Perhaps the wonderful healing power of Jesus, portrayed in this story, though impressive at the physical level, would also be taken to signify his healing power in situations of schism, when the body of believers was crippled by controversy. Perhaps Jesus' assertion of his authority over the religious/moral law, over the holy sabbath itself, would be even more amazing and significant to early Christians than his miraculous word-deed. Perhaps his implication that *his* attitude/action was the *real* fulfillment of the original commandment would be even stronger evidence of his role as spokesman and agent of God (son) han the astonishing manner in which he performed his ministry of *rest*oration.

There are three significant results of *Form Criticism* that affect the interpretation of the Gospel of Mark today.

(1) The first is the recognition that the book is not a continuously or sequentially composed document written by a single author. Rather it is a composition of numerous previously written smaller units and combinations of such units,[4] compiled by at least one "editor" (perhaps two)[5] who linked these separate parts together with connecting words and phrases, in a special order for the purpose of communicating his (or her)[6] particular, if not unique, understanding of the meaning of Jesus of Nazareth. The final editor-author also added—in addition to connecting words and phrases—summaries, and some original constructions. All of this, obviously, indicates that when we read the book of Mark we are actually reading the works of numerous different "authors," each with its layers of accumulated usage-meaning.

(2) The separate written units of tradition (parables, pronouncement [saying] stories, miracle stories, etc.) which were collected and connected by the redactor (or redactors) of this book, originated in oral form, circulated freely, were preserved, shaped, and reshaped as they were used in preaching, teaching, and worship, and were finally written down *in the early Christian communities* in Palestine and other parts of the Roman Empire during the period between the death of Jesus (ca. 31–33 A.D.) and the *composition* of this "Gospel" (ca. 65–75 A.D.). This fact strongly suggests that these units of tradition, individually or collectively, cannot be read unreservedly as objective, factual reports of words and acts of Jesus and objective, historical records of events occurring within the life of Jesus. The Gospel According to Mark certainly preserves some actual words and deeds of Jesus and some historical events pertaining to the life and death of Jesus. These, however, are imbedded within a generation of interpretation, proclamation, education, adoration, and expectation.

None of the documents of the New Testament (including the "Gospels" of Matthew, Mark, Luke, and John) are primarily, or even essentially, objective historical reports of bare facts. They are rather responses to, interpretations of, proclamations about the person of Jesus, his words spoken, his deeds done and the events which took place in a relatively short period (one to three years) at the end of his earthly life; they are witnesses to the definitive and continuing *meaning* of Jesus in the lives of believing individuals and groups after his death.

Therefore, when we read in the text of Mark, for example, that "Jesus said" this, or "Jesus did" that, or this particular event "took place" we must be aware that although there may be an actual historical occurrence originally behind this *declaration of meaning,* what we are actually reading now, primarily and essentially, is the end result of an extended process of symbolizing the *religious faith* of early Christians. In the Gospels, through the "forms," we learn as much or more about the beliefs, practices, problems, hopes, etc., of the early Christian church as we do about the historical person who is the subject of the Gospels and the object of the church's faith.[7]

(3) The final editor-authors or redactors[8] of the Gospels had specific reasons for choosing the sources which they used. The manner in which they decided to combine, change, and arrange them tell us something about their ideas, beliefs, and intentions as well as something about the situations in which they composed their documents and the situations of their originally intended recipients. This means that the final redactors of the Gospels were not merely casual collectors and combiners (like a person stringing different colored beads on a string in a random nonorder); but, rather, they were creative "authors" fashioning their materials into purposive patterns (arranging their different colored beads on the string in an intentional order). This means, further, that their final creations must each be read, viewed, and interpreted as a whole, in the way they created them, and in the way they intended them to be understood and experienced. Just as we must hear, interpret, and experience a Beethoven symphony not only in its various movements or parts with their individual themes, but also in its entirety as a total musical statement, so must we interpret a Gospel, such as Mark, not only by verses, forms, sections, etc., but also as a complete arrangement made up of composite religious themes resulting in an overall declaration of theological conviction.

Redaction Criticism grasped the importance of the implications of the insights in this third result of form criticism. Redaction criticism (or *Redaktionsgeschichte,* "redaction history," as the German scholars call it),[9] a relatively recent method in biblical study, seeks to determine the interpretive, or conceptual, or religious significance of the creative editorial activity of the redactor. This includes the manner in which the redactor combined the sources (forms, complexes or previously joined sections of material, etc.), provided introductions to stories, incidents, sayings, etc., arranged and adapted the separate units (e.g., enclosing one within two others in order to suggest an idea which the redactor held to be important),[10] composed and employed connecting words and phrases, constructed and inserted summaries, alloted space within limitations (e.g., the story of the last week of Jesus' life takes up about one-third of Mark's Gospel), and so forth. The degree to which the redaction critics are able to discern the editorial activity of the redactor-authors of the Gospels and its significance accurately is the degree to which they are able to suggest answers to questions like authorship, place of composition, date, motives for composition, and theological motifs, as these are reflected in the documents. This undertaking is easier with Matthew and Luke, because they both used Mark as a primary source, and by comparing and contrasting their texts with that of Mark it can be seen how they each have employed and modified distinctively their common source. With Mark it is necessary to discover, identify, and delineate the sources as well as to discern and interpret the work of the redactor(s), etc. Measurable progress has been made, but this task is far from complete.

Structural Exegesis combines insights from philosophy, psychology, anthropology, and linguistics in its interpretive approach to biblical documents. It does not ignore, but it is neither determined by nor confined to the results of the three disciplines described above. Its primary concern is to facilitate a meaningful *participation* in and personal *experience* of, not only the original intent of the author of a document, but also the subsequent and contemporary meanings generated by and communicated through the formal linguistic (literary) structures and processes (e.g., parables, myths, paradigms, narratives). It seeks to connect these meanings "existentially" with the total life experience of the interpreter.[11]

The methodology used in the analysis of Mark's document and the presentation of Mark's meaning in this exploration is primarily that of *redaction criticism* (as defined and described above) informed by the results and insights of *literary* (source) *criticism, form criticism,* and to a lesser extent *structural exegesis.* "Part II: St. Mark Speaks" is essentially a demonstration and application of the redaction-critical approach and an attempt to lead the reader into a first-hand experience of the redactional-theological activity of Mark as this expresses itself in three major themes and several underlying motifs: (1) Soteriology (Suffering and Salvation); (2) Christology (Titles for Jesus); (3) Eschatology (Final Fulfillment); the urgency of the faith (*euthus, eutheos*—immediately); the private *teaching of Jesus* and his command for silence about his identity; the *continuing* character of the Gospel.

"Part III: St. Mark Heard" presupposes the principles and insights of literary criticism, form criticism, redaction criticism, and structural exegesis. However, it presents some of the results of these methodologies, without exposing them quite so obviously, in a more familiar fashion. It consists of: (1) An interpretive essay "Christ and Conflict" which combines historical data, literary analysis, and theological reflection in a discussion of an (if not *the*) over-arching theme of the Gospel of Mark. Sub-sections of this essay are: "Conflict in the Cosmos," "Conflict in Palestine," "Conflict in Rome." (Within the third sub-section, "Conflict in Rome," questions of authorship, date, and provenance are dealt with briefly. Mark has already introduced these questions and their implications in his address, "Part II: St. Mark Speaks.") The attempt is made to translate the continuing and current theological-existential meanings of this three-fold theme from their first-century mythological categories of expression (the symbols of a three-storied supernatural universe) into categories of individual and corporate experience today. This attempt at translation is made through comments and questions within each of the three sub-sections named above, and more generally, within a fourth sub-section called "Conflict in Contemporary Culture." (2) Fourteen interpretive reflections interpreting representative passages from Mark's Gospel and attempting to suggest appropriate applications of Mark's meanings to contemporary life, individual and corporate, both within and without the church. In these more detailed and in-depth studies of specific sections of this document the methods and insights of literary criticism, form criticism, and biblical word-study play a more prominent part and become more apparent. However, the principles of redaction criticism and the insights of structural exegesis are not completely forgotten or totally abandoned. The numerous cross references between Parts II and III testify to their interrelatedness and to the fact that they somewhat overlap.

Now let us move into our thematic exploration of the Gospel of Mark, "Part II: St. Mark Speaks," employing primarily the techniques of redaction criticism. But on the way you are invited to pass through the portal of a "parabolic prolegomenon," i.e., a short fanciful story the purpose of which is to present in a form different from the usual prosaic explanation the rationale for the procedure in Parts II and III.

Anawatuk
in the Orange Grove

Once upon a time there was a young Eskimo named Anawatuk who lived in an igloo up near Noatok, Alaska. He had never seen a real orange. He had seen only pictures of oranges in posters about Florida which hung all over the walls of the general store in Noatok. The storekeeper had a thing about Florida. One day, having dogsledded into town Anawatuk went to the general store. There the storekeeper told him about a wonderful opportunity. The manufacturer of the cornmeal which Anawatuk occasionally bought was having a contest and the winner would receive a fantastic prize: a trip to Florida. All you had to do was sign your name and address to the form on the boxtop. With the help of the storekeeper, Anawatuk entered the contest. He won. He dogsledded to Fairbanks and caught the plane for Orlando. After a few days, Anawatuk, flat-busted, turned up hitchhiking along a highway near Winter Haven. He had blown all his money in the shows and on the rides at Disney World. That was where everybody had told him to *go first*. That was what they had told him to *do*. They had said that Disney World was really the place to see.

Anawatuk has now been walking along the highway without anything to eat or drink for almost two days and he is very tired, hungry, and thirsty. Not at all to our surprise he comes upon an orange grove and wanders in, at first just to lie down in the cool shade under one of the trees to rest. Lying there on his back he notices that the boughs of this tree above him are laden with big round orange things that look like the pictures of the fruit he has seen on the walls of the general store in Noatok. He thinks to himself, "There might be some nourishment in those things, something to help satisfy my hunger and quench my thirst. I wonder how I should go about getting it."

Orange grove strollers enter. Anawatuk, seeking helpful advice in his state of need, asks each one the same question, pointing to the oranges in the tree: "Are these things good to eat, is there any nourishment in them, and if so, how do you go about getting it?"

First orange grove stroller: "No, these things are *not* good to eat. They are an ancient, fossilized, unevolved, primitive, unscientifically produced, non-synthetic, and, therefore, non-nutritional so-called 'fruit.' So we just let them hang there until they fall to the ground and rot. You might use them for fertilizer or, when they dry out, for fuel, but nobody in his right mind would try to eat one or get any nourishment from one."

Second orange grove stroller: "Don't you know that you are in the sacred grove of the great god Sunkist? Why, these are holy oranges. They are the direct products of the divine rays of Sunkist's shining orb. You don't touch these oranges. You just look at them in awe and adoration of Sunkist. If you were to pick one and try to eat it, if you didn't drop dead immediately, you would find that its food is not for human consumption—it is purely divine—fit for the 'holy' only. And in any case, Sunkist doesn't like people picking his oranges! So keep your dirty hands off!"

Third orange grove stroller: "Sure you can eat these things! Yes, this is the sacred orange grove of the great god Sunkist; but he produced these oranges *for* human consumption, to satisfy human hunger and quench human thirst. There's only one thing: since they are holy oranges produced directly by the sacred rays of the holy Sunkist you must eat them in a proper holy way. The only way approved of by Sunkist is *not to pick them at all*. You don't touch them with your unclean hands. First, you wash your mouth seven times with holy water from the sacred irrigation ditch right over there. Those two men standing guard there will show you how. Then you just come to the tree, stand on your tiptoes, if necessary, clasp your hands behind your back, and bite right into the orange (if you can)."

Anawatuk was *very* hungry and thirsty so he did exactly as this grove stroller told him. Having gone through the lengthy mouth-washing ritual and finally gotten the orange in a position with his nose and lips so he could take a bite—he bit! And he ate! Even though the rind was bitter and burned his lips and the citrus oil squirted in his eyes and smarted them. In fact, it was only a few minutes after eating it that the holy orange made him very sick. His stomach ached terribly. He thought maybe that went along with getting the wonderful nourishment from holy oranges so he tried not to complain. But after awhile he could hold it down no longer.

Fourth orange grove stroller: "Yes, these oranges *are* good to eat. They were produced ultimately by Sunkist for human nourishment. But the trees were planted, cultivated, irrigated, pruned, and sprayed by humans. These oranges, therefore, are the result of a combined creativity on the part of both Sunkist and human beings. They contain lots of Vitamin C. This comes from the great god Sunkist and it is essential for human health. But in order to get this nourishment it is necessary to pick the orange and peel it, if you wish to eat the meat of the fruit while getting the juice. Or, you can cut the orange open and squeeze it to get the juice out. The *juice* is the main thing. There is not much human food value in the pulp or the little membrane sacs which hold the juice. (The rind, as you *know*, is not easily digestible!) So if you are going to peel one and eat it, it's probably better to pull it apart and put it in your mouth section by section. That way you will get most of the juice. While you are doing this you should notice how wonderfully and beautifully each orange is constructed, how the sections are joined by connective tissue, how all fit together in the spherical pattern to make the delightful, delicious, and nourishing whole. If you notice all this while you are taking the fruit apart section by section, believe it or not it will taste better, you will appreciate it more, it will be more easily digestible. And, some people say, it will even be more nourishing. If you just munch right into the whole orange from any angle the juice is likely to squirt out all over the place, even run out the corners of your mouth and down your chin. Here, let me show you. I'll help you."

So Anawatuk was nourished and learned how to peel and break apart oranges in order to eat them and how to squeeze them in order to get their juice. The strange and wonderful thing about these oranges, however, was that they were not destroyed by the peeling, eating, cutting, and squeezing. They kept reappearing on the tree whole and fresh and full of nourishment, ripe and ready for any who were willing to exert the time and effort required to obtain the basic skills needed to get at this nourishment.

PART II:

St. Mark

A Short Explanatory Note from the Author

In "Part II: St. Mark Speaks," I am trying to give you a *feel* for how the Gospel of Mark came into existence, how its "author" (final redactor, the person who put it together in the form in which we now read it in the New Testament) composed it, and some of the motives, intentions, main ideas, basic concerns, religious themes, definitive personal-community beliefs, convictions, and commitments underlying its composition.

I am attempting to present some of the fundamental "insights" (generally accepted and currently agreed upon by many New Testament Scholars) about the composition, character, and Christian faith reflected in this document, *through an imaginary first person report by the author.*[1]

Before we hear St. Mark "tell it like it was," we should remember that the identity of the final author is unknown to us. We're not even sure whether Mark was a female or a male. There is, *possibly,* a pro-female attitude expressed in this book which *could* point to a female composer.[2] But lacking any non-Markan documentary support for, and with much against the thesis of a Marcia rather than a Mark[3] the character about to speak will be a male, and from now on, the author of our document will be referred to as "he," "him," etc.

We might also recognize that there is a place for at least a touch of humor in religion, indeed in Christianity, even in biblical scholarship, in fact in serious writing of introductions, commentaries, and guides to Gospels.[4] I

Speaks

know some interpreters have suggested that there was a narrow gate in the wall of Jerusalem in Jesus' day called "the needle's eye." But I still get a chuckle when I read Mark 10:25. Even if Jesus did not quote that old saying himself and it entered the Gospel tradition later, I feel confident that those who heard it or read it laughed, or at least smiled. If they were in a group standing or sitting around together I would not be surprised if a few of them (especially the poor, and there were plenty of those) guffawed and elbowed one another in the ribs, before they got straight-faced again.

Finally, footnotes can be informative and suggestive. Most of those used in this book are confined to Parts I and II. They are not absolutely essential for the meaning of what you are reading. But I hope you will find them interesting and helpful. So that they won't distract you while you are reading, I have removed them from the bottom of the pages and collected them all at the back of the book.

If you get the feeling while reading this book that you are meeting some of the same ideas in different places do not be surprised. You are. That is, I think, inevitable in the study of the Gospel of Mark. For the "author" of this document himself presents and re-presents some of the same basic themes again and again through the specific sources he uses (stories and sayings plus their meanings), arrangement of the material, editorial devices, and the overall structure of the document. Now let us go listen to what St. Mark has to tell us.

The Setting for St. Mark's Address

In order to provide an appropriate setting for our imaginary address from St. Mark, let us picture in our mind's eye a scene in which we can place ourselves: We are in a large auditorium at a college situated in an urban center. Gathered this evening in the hall are students and professors from the college; most are Christian; many would make no claim to be. Some of the students and professors of literature, philosophy and religion, from a state university nearby are in the audience. Also present in significant numbers are ministers from the city's churches, rabbis from the synagogues, laypersons from the congregations. Some adults of various ages and from various walks of life who have no personal or formal relation to institutional religion are here. Perhaps some of the theological students and some of their professors from a seminary within the community have come to be present for this occasion.

Since we have no reliable knowledge of the physical appearance of St. Mark,[5] I will refrain from suggesting any here. You may picture him as you wish. A professor in the department of religion has been asked to make the introduction. He and the guest speaker are sitting in chairs on the stage near the lectern and microphone. Unable to conceive of any adequate way to introduce the speaker, the professor simply rises and announces to the persons assembled: "Ladies and Gentlemen, St. Mark." St. Mark rises, steps forward to the lectern and, without notes, begins to speak.

ST. MARK'S ADDRESS

Ladies and gentlemen:

I greatly appreciate your invitation to be one of the speakers in your "Ancient Religious Documents" series. I wish I could stay to hear brothers Matthew, Luke, and John deliver their lectures.

Many "Saints"

You have asked me to tell you briefly how I composed "my" Gospel. I'll be glad to do that; but first I want to clear up this *saint* Mark business. I am no more saintly than many of you are. I agree with Paul that *all* who are related to God by grace through faith, through our Lord Jesus Christ, are saints.[6] It's not always possible, it's never easy, to know or decide who the saints are. That was one of the problems I was addressing when I composed the first Gospel. With this in mind read the following passages: Mark 11:12–25; 7:24–37; 8:27; 13:10.[7] Matthew really emphasized this point. Read what he recorded about verbal professions of faith and active obedience in love (Matt. 6:21–23; 25:31–46) and his startling parable of the wedding feast (Matt. 22:1–10). John Calvin reminded you a long time ago that the visible church is not always the true church and that the invisible true church does not always coincide with the visible church. Some who are on the rolls of the visible church may not be saints. And certainly there are some, if not many, saints among those who do not belong to the visible church (cf. Mark 14:9; 15:29).

Incidentally, I hope you brought a copy of the Bible with you, because I'm going to be making references to my Gospel (and other books in the Bible) by citing the chapter and verse numbers as these now appear in your English translations. You probably already know that when I put my Gospel together, and when it was copied by hand for hundreds of years after that, there were no chapter and verse divisions. In fact, when I first wrote my Gospel the words and sentences were not even separated, and there was no punctuation.[8] Papyrus was scarce and expensive. We could not waste space. So we just wrote, compiled, and copied letter after letter close to one another.

The separation of the letters into words, sentences, and paragraphs was done by copiest-editors much later. The division of the Gospel content into chapters and verses was begun, perhaps, by Eusebius, the church historian and bishop of Caesarea in the fourth century A.D. The first English version of the whole Bible to use numbered verses was the Geneva Bible of 1560.[9]

Many "Authors"

The original copy of my Gospel had no title; that also was added later. Nor did I sign my name to my first edition. I did not even think of doing that. In the first place I knew that "my" Gospel was not really *mine,* at least not mine alone. I was using stories, sayings, and combinations of these which had been handed down orally and used and shaped within the Christian communities for years by numerous people, many of whom I did not even know. I chose the ones I put together from those that were available to me. Some were still in oral form. Most had already been written down as separate units of the tradition (some of your scholars call them forms) and were being employed in Christian congregations in preaching, teaching, and worship. They also served to encourage, comfort, and exhort the people in times of distress.

Some of my material originated in Palestine and some of

it was created outside of Palestine in churches in both the Eastern and the Western parts of the Roman Empire. So, you see, in a real sense my Gospel is a corporate effort, an end result of a long process (from about 33 A.D. to about 65–75 A.D.), a community product. Naturally, I am not even sure of the origin of some of my material or the names of its original authors.

Anonymity

In the second place I *intended* to remain anonymous. I wanted *the message* I was attempting to communicate and *the person* who is the subject of that message to receive all the attention. That was what was important. I could add nothing to the significance of my message or that person by signing the document.[10] On the other hand my identity as the "author" might have detracted from it for some people. That I did *not* want. However, since it's the name by which I have been known for centuries, you may call me Mark (*Markos* in Greek, *Marcus* in Latin). This was a very common name in the Roman Empire during the first century.[11] Remember Marcus Aurelius and Mark Anthony?

The Traditional Mark

As many of you know, for over fifteen hundred years I have been identified by many scholars with a man named Mark who was said to have been an "interpreter" of or, perhaps, "secretary-companion" to the Apostle Peter.[12] Your New Testament scholars have documented this identification as far back as brother Eusebius, the fourth century church historian and bishop of Caesarea. Eusebius lived ca. 263–340 A.D. In Book Three, Section 39.15 of his *Ecclesiastical History* Eusebius, quoting from another Christian bishop named Papias (Bishop of Hierapolis) who had lived and written, presumably, in the first quarter of the second century, wrote:

> And this also the elder (presbyter) used to say. Mark was the interpreter of Peter and wrote down accurately, though not in order, that which he remembered of what was said or done by the Lord. He had, of course, neither heard the Lord nor did he follow him, but later, as I said, Peter. The latter adapted his teaching to the needs of the moment, but not as if he wanted to make a compilation of the Lord's sayings, so that Mark made no mistake when he wrote down some things as he remembered them. He intended only one thing, to omit or falsify nothing which he had heard.[13]

Now, quite obviously, according to Eusebius, Papias is quoting here from an "elder" or "presbyter." The Greek word he uses is *presbuteros*. Furthermore, according to Eusebius, Papias also claims in his writing *Sayings of the Lord Interpreted* "that he above all had investigated the oral tradition of the Lord, and had ascertained what the presbyters and the disciples of the Lord had said, and what Aristion and the presbyter John, the Lord's disciples were saying (Eus., EH III, 39, 3f.)."[14] In all probability the "elder" or "presbyter" referred to at the beginning of Papias' statement about Mark (above) is this same presbyter John.[15]

One of your fine New Testament scholars, Professor Achtemeier, has neatly summarized the significance of the "Papias Tradition" derived from brother Eusebius' History:

> Papias is there identified as one who knew people who had known the apostles; he thus belonged to the "third generation" of Christians. Eusebius recounts what Papias said he learned from Aristion and John the Elder (who are otherwise unknown), namely that the author of our Gospel was Mark who had been Peter's "interpreter" (it could also mean a kind of secretary-companion), and that he, Mark, wrote what he remembered of the things the Lord said and did (apparently from hearing Peter talk about those things), though he did not put them "in order" ... This tradition lies at the basis of our ascription of our Gospel to "Mark," since later traditions about the author clearly depend upon this tradition from Papias. In fact, succeeding generations of Christians linked Mark ever more closely with Peter, having Mark write during Peter's lifetime and finally at Peter's direction. That is simply an attempt to tie the Gospel ever more closely to an apostle so that apostolic authority could be claimed for it. In a similar way, tradition linked the author of the third Gospel, Luke, ever more closely with Paul. The basic insights of form criticism concerning the traditional nature of the Markan material constitute the chief argument against Papias' notion that the author of the second Gospel had been a companion of Peter.[16]

Numerous of your scholars have suggested that there are some "hints in the Gospel itself" that refer to the author. For example, "the seemingly pointless reference to the young man at the time of Jesus' arrest (14:51–52)."[17] Even if these references are such "hints" about me they, obviously, don't give my name or much revealing information about me. No, when all is said, I remain anonymous. And that's just fine with me. Because who I was biographically is not nearly as important as who I was "existentially." I mean my identity in terms of my religious exprience, my Christian beliefs, my life concerns, and my personal commitments.

The Real Mark Stands Up

Now let me *really* introduce myself. I'm a first century Christian who was completely convinced that Jesus had been raised from the dead (8:31; 9:9, 30–32; 14:28; 16:1–8), that he was alive, present, speaking and acting within the Christian communities and through individual Christians (13:11, 16:7), and that he was "coming again" soon to consummate the meaning of his life, death, and resurrection, to visibly establish his "kingdom" (chapter 13). I was also convinced that the definitive way Jesus had accomplished his purpose was through suffering unto crucifixion (1:11, 20; 3:6; 8:31–9:1; 9:2–13, 31; 10:29–31, 32–34, 45; 14:17–25, 32–42; 15:16–39).

I was further convinced that only through suffering could a Christian be a faithful follower of Jesus; or, to express that more accurately, any person who was a believer in Jesus' words and deeds and the meaning of his life and death, verified in his resurrection (16:1–8), and who faithfully followed him (as a disciple) would inevitably have to face and go through suffering in this world (e.g., 8:31–9:1; 10:35–45; 13:9–13).

I was concerned that individual Christians and congregations *not* forget the humanity of Jesus in an exclusive or excessive emphasis on his deity, i.e, our faith in his resurrection, his living spiritual presence among us, his ultimate authority over us, and his imminent future return (parousia 9:1; 13:20, 23, 26f., 29–31; 14:25). Or to put that another way, my understanding of and participation in the story of Jesus, my response to the Gospel, the "saving" action of God in and through Jesus (e.g., 1:14f., 13:10; 14:9), while resolving fundamental conflicts within human existence did not remove me from history, time, space, physical embodiment, or involvement in this world. On the contrary, it sent me into the world to announce this "good news" (cf. 1:1; 3:13–15; 6:7–13). Furthermore, belief in the resurrection of Jesus and his return in the near future, plus being "in Christ" by faith in the present, did not mean, as some of my brothers and sisters thought, being on a constant religious "high." Nor did being spirit-filled, enthusiastically[18] related to the risen Jesus Christ, celebrated especially in the sacrament of the Lord's Supper it imply non-conflicting, tensionless removal or escape from the unreal world of everyday life.

So my purpose in composing and publishing my "Gospel" in the form that I did was not only positively proclamatory; it was also partly corrective. You see, some of my brothers and sisters in the faith were, understandably, caught up in the "release" they experienced in their new individual relationships to God through the event of Jesus. They were so enthused about the community they felt with one another and with him in a spiritual sense, and in the power of his personal presence, particularly during the celebration of the eucharist, that they were making extravagant claims about presently sharing in the wonderful divine "dynamis" (power) of the Lord (see 1 Cor. 11–14, especially 11:17–12:31; Mark 9:2–13; 13; 14:12–41; 15:1–39).[19] One problematic manifestation of this enthusiasm was speaking in tongues (1 Cor. 12–14).

An Unfinished Drama That Continues

One thing I earnestly wanted to communicate to these people through "my Gospel" was that the divine drama, though decisively defined in the life, death, and resurrection of Jesus, were not finally finished. Though he was coming back soon, the Lord hadn't returned *yet* (e.g., 13)! Therefore, our attitude and our action were to be that of watchful waiting (13:32–37; 14:37–38), faithful obedience (8:27–9:1; 10:17–31, 35–45), trust in the love of God and care for our brothers and sisters in the faith (3:34–35; 10:15, 43; 12:28–34; 8:34–9:1).

I chose to communicate this conviction to my first readers by selecting from all those that were being circulated stories and sayings which stated these beliefs. Another method I employed (which your redaction critics have discovered) involved careful attention to the sequence in the arrangement of my material. For example, immediately *before* the story of the transfiguration I put Jesus' teaching that "'the Son of Man must suffer'" and that if any persons would come after Jesus let them deny themselves, take up their crosses and follow him (8:31, 34–38). Immediately after this story of the otherworldly, mountain-top experience (possibly a resurrection story in its original form, 9:2–8), I put the descent back into the valley of the shadow of death (9:9–13), including the specific reminder that as it is "written of the Son of Man... he should suffer many things and be treated with contempt." (9:12) In other words, by placing material about this world suffering before and after the transfiguration, I provided important clues about the meaning of the transfiguration scene.

Also, although I included obvious anticipations of the resurrection (8:31; 9:9, 31; 14:28) and the clear announcement of its occurrence (16:6), I purposefully left my story incomplete (16:6–8). I intended to imply by the abrupt stop, as if in the middle of a sentence,[20] that the story "was being continued and was to be concluded." Some early readers thought that either I had not finished my manuscript in the first place or else the original ending had been lost, and so, they provided it with an ending. There are two main versions of this, a shorter and a longer one, which you can read in *The Oxford Annotated Bible* (p. 1238). Some modern scholars have also thought that my original document (scroll) had somehow lost its conclusion.[21]

The Main Subject and Four Preliminary Remarks

Already I've gotten pretty far into my main subject, the primary thing you wanted me to share with you, as I understood your request: how I put my Gospel together, what some of my most important concerns or themes were, and how I expressed these themes through the structure of my document. I've just given one illustration. But now I think I should get more organized. So what I'll do is this: I will briefly state the theme, list some of the passages—in many cases these were separate units of material which I inherited—which communicate or reflect the theme, and then I will explain how I put specific sections or blocks of material together in such a way as to suggest the meaning of this theme. I will do this only for three of the most important and obvious themes. I cannot discuss them all now, nor will I go into many details. Rather I will try to give you the big picture on each of the ones I select. Following this I will indicate briefly how I put the whole document together. Finally I will suggest an appropriate overall outline in case you wish to use it for studying my Gospel.

But just a few more incidental remarks before we take up these themes and structures one by one. First, although it may sound thus far as though I merely used the cut-and-paste method, and although I was heavily dependent upon what I received through the oral traditions and the separate units of written material, I did also include in my composite "Gospel" some sayings and stories which were preserved particularly in my community, as well as the connectives, introductions, and summaries (some of which I will cite later) which I wrote myself.

Secondly, this whole process of analysis which you are following in taking the document apart in order to better comprehend its meaning, though quite legitimate and perhaps even necessary today, nevertheless feels rather strange to me. I would have never thought that *you* would ever be doing it!

When I first composed my Gospel I assumed that anyone who read it, or listened to it would understand my overall message and recognize the importance of the sub-themes and the shades of meaning expressed by my method (the particular selection of material I made, my connections, introductions, summaries, arrangements, etc.). I assumed that those who first received my Gospel were familiar with much of the content of the material, the ideas or themes which were being stated in various ways, and the structural techniques which I employed. I knew that they were accustomed to the nonliteral or symbolic mode of expressing religious truth. They didn't make the sharp distinction which you modern-minded people make between the literal and the nonliteral, the objective scientific fact and the subjective symbolic meaning, the natural and the supernatural. Also, generally speaking, they had more of a sense of the dramatic, the representative, suggestive, meaningful significance of places, persons, and actions; the telling character of movements (shifts, turns, changes) that occur in a story. They did not ask first off the question: "Did it actually happen like that?" Rather they entered into the play, the dramatic-story and mentally and emotionally participated in it, in order to experience its intended, personal, and ultimately *real* meaning. I also assumed that my original readers or hearers (most people could not read and write back in those days) would catch the significant meanings I was attempting to communicate through my creative editing, my juxtaposing, combining, bracketing sayings and stories. They were accustomed to this kind of thing in their oral (and written) folk stories, poems, songs, and plays.

Maybe one reason why it is difficult, sometimes, for you

moderns to understand the Bible and other ancient religious documents, and necessary for us to do this kind of analysis as a part of interpretation, is that you think, feel, read, and hear differently from the way my people did. Therefore a lot more explanation is needed for you than was necessary for first-century folks. I suppose in order to really "get it" you people are going to have to try to think, feel, read, and hear as they did and then translate the meaning you get into the language of your world, your experience, your life.

Thirdly, and this is connected to what I just said, I hope you people are coming to appreciate the appropriateness as well as the philosophical profundity of writing theology, claims and convictions about ultimate truth and meaning, in the form of a *story*. The idea of religion as story, or biography, or even autobiography is currently being explored (again) by numerous of your capable scholars.[22] It was one of the ways we did theology *naturally*. For example: Homer's *Iliad* and *Odyssey,* the Greek myths, Old Testament legends and stories, Jewish Rabbinic parables, the parables of Jesus. (Another common way was to write letters. See, for example, those of Paul in the New Testament.) However, I must quickly add here, that my Gospel is not a full biography, nor is it a historical novel. It's definitely not a tape recording, or a movie, or a stenographer's write-up, or a newsperson's report.

As a Gospel my document is more like a short story or a short play. But I didn't have any precise literary form to go by as an artistic precedent.[23] I decided upon this particular form, which later came to be called Gospel (partly because of the first sentence of my document which *can* be read as a title), for several reasons.[24] Some of Paul's letters were circulating around the Roman Empire, mostly within Christian congregations. In most cases they were written to specific church situations, answering particular questions, addressing certain problems, etc. Paul definitely communicated what he believed about God (theology), human nature (anthropology), Christ (Christology), salvation (soteriology), etc., through these letters, sometimes in a more (Romans), sometimes a less (1 and 2 Corinthians) systematic way. But he didn't use many sayings of the Lord or stories about him, and often his language was fairly sophisticated, in places you might even say abstract (e.g., Rom. 3:21–8:39).

Well, I thought several things: the form I decided upon

would be a different means of communicating the Christian faith, as well as correcting some mistaken ideas. As a dramatic-story form it might be easier to understand, to remember, than epistles or letters. Also it would preserve more of the important sayings and teachings of our Lord as well as some of the important stories about his acts and about events which took place during the definitive period of his life, the last year or so. I thought this was particularly urgent because those first followers of Jesus were dying off, passing from our midst, and soon we could no longer hear these stories and sayings from their own lips. Also, I thought maybe this Gospel form might catch people's attention and evoke personal identification with the Lord through imaginative participation in the story. Most of us common folk back in those days delighted in and responded enthusiastically to this kind of presentation of meaning. I thought it would make an effective evangelistic tract, evoke a positive response to its word-picture message. As a literary form it is consistent with and reflects what happened. Because what *happened* was a human-devine drama story; and that drama-story continues to happen, even through the written form! Also, I thought that individual brothers and sisters as well as congregations in situations of distress, persecution, or conflict would get my message in this form and in it find support, comfort, reassurance, guidance, and strength.

Fourthly, before we delineate some of my themes and structural patterns, I want to share this thought with you. I didn't know I was divinely inspired when I composed my Gospel.[25] I was just doing, as a committed and concerned Christian, what I thought should be done. I suppose you might call it an act of love and devotion, if you include in that description the simple awareness of, and the attempt to meet, what were perceived to be serious, if not urgent, needs. Honestly, I had no idea that I was producing "holy writ," or "sacred scripture." It's perfectly all right with me if that is what it came to be considered under the guidance of the Spirit in the church. But I thought I would just tell you that I didn't go into a trance during which the whole thing was revealed to me directly by divine dictation, or that even without the trance I felt special divine revelation coming through me. I *did* believe it was God's will that I compose and send forth my Gospel. And I did so to the best of my ability. But the way *I* experienced it, it was a very human work. I'm glad that God has used it as an effective medium for his message; but I wanted to say this for two reasons. One, in the hope that it would enable some of you to approach my Gospel more openly and receptively; and, two, because I think this is a further illustration of one of my major themes: the divine and the human are not so dichotomous, not so radically and definitely separate. Indeed, it is in, with, and through the *Human* (Jesus) that the *Divine* Person, Will, and Action are disclosed.

Now we had better get on to those themes, my personal additions, and that outline. The first major motif which I composed into my Gospel and which I want to explore with you is the motif of suffering.

Soteriology

The fact that suffering and salvation are inseparable both for Savior and disciple was one of my basic convictions, one of the fundamentals of my faith. Indeed, it was one of those definitive experience-beliefs of my Christian community. I will say a little more about that community shortly. But right now I just want to state this theme briefly, then illustrate how I wove it into the tapestry of my Gospel.

I'm reluctant to use the word "theme," however, because I'm afraid it might connote to you an objective concept that somebody thought up and then wrote into a thesis. That's not it at all. This theme is a deep and strongly held conviction of both head and heart, rooted in what we had heard, what we held in faith and what we were experiencing in our lives.[26]

But before I get into it any further I feel compelled to remind you that we first-century Christians were not speculating about what we had not experienced when we talked about suffering. There was real conflict for Christians not only in Palestine and Rome, but also, generally, throughout our world. The persecutions, calamities, suffering, etc., to which I refer in chapter 13 (a crucial chapter in my book) were not confined to one place or the other, or to a specific time. Of course, they were more concentrated at certain times and places than at others. For example, they were particularly intense during the Roman repression of the Jewish revolt and the destruction of the Jerusalem temple in 66–70 A.D. (cf. 13:7–8, 14) and the persecution of Christians by the emperor Nero in Rome in 63 A.D.[27]

This theme, "Suffering and Salvation Are Inseparable,"

goes like this: contrary to the main stream of Hebrew-Jewish expectation which held that divine deliverance would come through political power, military might, or supernatural spectacular intervention,[28] the divinely appointed agent of God for the deliverance of his people (and ultimately *all* people) *must,* indeed *did,* bring this deliverance-salvation about through suffering—even unto death by crucifixion. All those who faithfully follow this savior can expect and must be prepared for suffering like his, possibly death, because of him and his gospel (cf. 1:1, 14; 2:2; 4:17).

The other side of this suffering and dying is *real* living, both for Savior and disciple. The suffering and dying for the disciple may not always be physical. It may be psychological, or spiritual, or relational. It *may* mean an identity crisis, a turning away from an old mode of mere existence, and a choosing of a new mode of vital being with all the difficulties, stresses, and strains this entails (e.g., 1:16–20; 10:29–31). It may mean letting go of ways of believing and acting that are rigid and deadly, and vulnerably embracing a new, open, and vital way of faith (2:23–3:6; 7:1–8, 14–23; 12:28–34). It may, painfully but inevitably, cause the parting of ways with family and friends over what is ultimately true and valuable and claiming in one's life, unto one's death, with all the sorrow, sadness, and solitude this brings with it (3:31–35; 10:28–31; 13:12–13). All this leads to joyful life, partially now and perfectly in the swiftly coming new age, when the Lord will complete this divine eschatalogical drama, this passion play, of the end of the old world and the realization of the new community of God. But there is no shortcut around suffering and death to get there. At the same time, as paradoxical as this may sound, the community of the faithful followers of Jesus anticipates and participates in the life of the new age (by faith) even in this old world of suffering and death right now. The quality of our present existence is defined by what God has accomplished through Jesus (past) and the character of the future new age.

Now that you know that urgently stating, effectively communicating, creatively and dramatically presenting this theme was one of the motives, perhaps the primary motive, for me to compose my Gospel, you can pick up my tract and read through it and discern for yourself how this bold red thread is woven so prominently throughout the whole fabric of my work. (Incidentally, this metaphor of the tapestry, or this extended simile comparing my Gospel to a weaving, is, I think a good and appropriate one. In a tapestry all the different designs and color motifs are interwoven to make the whole fabric, all are connected or interrelated, and while some stand out and others are more subtle yet each depends on all, with overlapping and repetition; so are the themes expressed in my Gospel).

But rather than leave you totally to your own devices, let's take a quick look at some of the ways I wove this bold red theme into my tapestry. If you would like to do it for yourself before I give you some hints, that would be great! Here are some verses and sections (passages) which I think you will find pertinent. Why don't you read these and ponder their singificance as individual warp and weft interlacings together creating this design which is being prominently woven into the whole fabric, before I say anything else?

Mark 1:1–3 related to 1:9–11. (I can't resist making one suggestion here: Remember that it was our custom a long time ago to quote just one verse or two, or maybe just a couple of words or a phrase, from a whole passage in order to recall the whole passage and its meaning. Also we sometimes juxtaposed [or combined] two or more such references to form a new meaning). Pause briefly at 1:24; 2:6f.; 2:15–17, 18–22 (esp. 2:20); 2:23–3:6; 3:21–29; *4:17; 6:14–29, 34; *8:27–33; *8:34–9:1; 9:2–8 connected to 9:9–14; 9:30–32; 9:49; 10:1; 10:28–31; 10:32–34; 10:35–45; 11:1–10; 12:1–12; 13: esp. vss. 9–13; 14:1–2; 14:3–9; 14:10–15:47. (An asterisk placed before any scripture reference is an indication of emphasis.)

Well, that's most of my book, isn't it? That should give you an idea about how central, even key, this motif is. What did you feel as you read through these passages? Did you sense that the big clue was given and the tone set early in the story and that it kept surfacing, pushing its way to the center of the stage until it totally occupied the spotlight, became the major theme, and brought the drama to its climax in the crucifixion? (15:39: "And when the centurian, who stood facing him, saw that he thus breathed his last, he said, 'Truly this man was the son of God!' ")

Perhaps you noticed that what many scholars and most Christians have traditionally called the Passion Week (or the

Passion Narrative) consumes chapters 11–15 with the resurrection taking up 16, just about one-third of my document. That should tip off the reader to the climactic and definitive importance this act, with its several scenes, carries in my drama. I did intend to suggest a seven-day scenario. However, if you read through these chapters carefully, looking for clear designations of exactly seven days, and specific places, you probably recognized that I was not concerned with strict chronology or precise geography; nor was the traditional material I was using. I was concerned with soteriology, the saving significance of Christ in conflict until crucifixion (specifically in Jerusalem)! Recall, e.g., the placement of time references and the vagueness of some that occur (11:1, 11, 12, 20, 27; 12:1, 13, 18, 35; 13:1, 3; *14:1, 12; 15:1, 16, *33, 34, 42), the feeling of uncertainty about where the action is taking place in several cases (e.g., 11:20; 12:1, 13, 18; 14:12), and how Jesus and his disciples get from one place to another.[29]

I'm sure you felt the action slow down, become more deliberate and detailed in chapters 14–16. These chapters portray only the last two (or three?) days of Jesus' earthly life. Yet they consume about one-sixth of the total papyrus on my scroll! These two chapters are about "Jesus' Being Anointed (for his burial, 14:8) at Bethany (14:3–9), "The Last Supper" (14:12–25), "The Prediction of the Disciples' Betrayal and Peter's Denial" (14:26–31), "Jesus' Struggle in Gethesemane" (14:32–42), "Jesus' Betrayal by Judas" (14:10–11, 17–21, 41–42, 43–50), "Jesus' Trial before the High Priest (Caiaphas) and the Council" (14:53–65), "Peter's Denial" (14:66–72), "Jesus' Trial before Pilate" (15:1–5), "The Choice of the Crowd between Jesus and Barabbas and Pilate's Deliverance of Jesus to Be Crucified" (15:6–15), "The Mocking of Jesus" (15:16–20), "The Crucifixion" (15:21–41), and "The Burial (15:42–47) of Jesus."

I didn't intend to divide these two chapters (14 and 15) into their composite parts and describe their content just now. But it's just as well, because by so doing I have made even more obvious that this last third of my book (11–16) is characterized by conflict, trial, tribulation, suffering, and death, as *necessary* foreword to resurrection and new life. There is a sense in which, as in one of your modern mystery novels, it is necessary to know the conclusion of my story before you can fully understand what's happening as it unfolds from the beginning. You need to read it from beginning to end, then from end to beginning (and back again!) in order to really get it as it was intended to be read and understood. Most of my original readers/hearers knew this because they already knew the climax (15) and the to-be-continued conclusion (16). Those in my religious community also shared the belief in its message, which is stated in part in this "theme."

But let's go back quickly now to the beginning and read those passages I listed briefly describing what's being said.

Right off I use the designation of Jesus Christ as "the Son of God." I won't go into the possible meanings of that appellation of Jesus, because I am going to talk about the titles for Jesus that appear in my Gospel in more detail shortly. I will simply say that in our early original *Jewish*-Christian thought and usage it did not signify a divine being (or god-man, a common Greek and pagan mid-Eastern idea), but rather a divinely (God)-appointed person, a representative or active agent of God. But the main thing to notice is how I define, by association, by accumulative implication, through Old Testament references and other words, my understanding of the *way*, or the *modus operandi* of *this* Son of God, i.e., *how* he *is*, and *acts*, and functions as the Son who brings about the Father's deliverance of his family (cf. 1:1, 11; 3:11; 5:7; 9:7; 12:6f.; 14:61; 15:39; 3:35).

Immediately after announcing that this is "the beginning of the gospel of Jesus Christ, the Son of God," I begin to signal that he and the gospel about him are the fulfillment of Hebrew hopes, prophetic predictions and promises but in a different, redefined sense. Chapter 1, verse 2 is taken from Malachi 3:1. In this passage Malachi is announcing that a prophetic messenger has appeared to " 'prepare the way before' " the Lord who will " 'suddenly come to his temple' " (the authoritative and symbolic center of Israel–Judaism) to bring judgment against those forces which oppose his sovereign authority and those persons who violate his holy will (Mal. 3:1–5) and to create a new community out of the minority who repent, change their ways, and relate to God according to his original life-giving and life-sustaining covenant (Mal. 3:2–4, 6, 16–18; 4:1–5). Malachi 4:5 says: " 'Behold, I will send you Elijah the prophet before the great and terrible day of the LORD comes.' " Like other early Christian evangelists and teachers, I identified John the Baptist, respresentatively, with Elijah (e.g., 9:11–13; see also Matt. 11:13–15). resentative of the Father to speak his word and act on his behalf; John the Baptist is "Elijah" who sets the stage for "God's Act." It is the final act, the end (the Greek word for end or goal is *eschaton*), the "eschatological event," the denouement of the drama, the finale (which will inaugurate a new scene). This involves judgment, a separation of the true from the untrue, the faithful from the unfaithful, the obedient from the disobedient. Now another image is added. Verse 3 of chapter 1 is a quote from Isaiah, 40:3. This whole passage (Isa. 40:1–11) is about the coming of God as deliverer, savior, redeemer, and about making a new Exodus across the desert (vss. 3–5), releasing the people from captivity, terminating warfare, and forgiving sin—"Comfort, comfort my people, says your God." (Isa. 40:1) This "savior God" is pictured as a conquering king (Isa. 40:10). But here, also, a modification of the typical military monarch occurs. He is described as a shepherd who with strength, but also with gentleness and tenderness, cares for his flock (Isa. 40:11).

Jesus, "the Christ," "the Son of God" is being identified by association with the symbolic figures in these prophetic oracles and the divine action which they denote.

We make our meaning even more apparent, for the reader or hearer who knows his or her Old Testament, in the story of Jesus' baptism in 1:9–11. This is a big tip-off about how we understand Jesus and the first really obvious weaving in of this bold red design of salvation through suffering. In 1:11 there is a combination of phrases from Psalm 2:7 ("You are my son" = Mark 1:11*b*: "Thou art my beloved Son") and Isaiah 42:1 ("in whom my soul delights" = Mark 1:11*c*: "with thee I am well pleased"). Psalm 2 is about a mighty king of Israel who conquers the enemies of Israel and, as God's representative, symbolizes the sovereignty and saving power of God. Isaiah 42:1–4, on the other hand, is a poem about "the servant of the Lord" (Lord = Yahweh, Israel's special name for God), who with the spirit (breath, life, vital power) of the Lord upon him brings forth "justice to the nations" by non-agressive, non-violent means. This poem (Isa. 42:1–4) is the first of a cycle of four "Servant Songs" (Isa. 42:1–4; 49:1–6; 50:4–11; 52:13–53:12) in 2 Isaiah (Isaiah 40–55, "the prophet of the exile") which depict an agent of God as enacting his will (justice, restoration of relationship to the Lord, as "'a light to the nations, that my salvation may reach to the end of the earth,'" [Isa. 49:6] etc.). This representative of God accomplishes God's will by suffering, indeed vicarious suffering unto death—non-aggressive, non-resistant suffering in the place of, in the stead of others. This is "the Servant of the Lord" (Isa. 42:1; 49:3; 50:10; 52:13) who "was bruised for our iniquities," upon whom "was the chastisement that made us whole, and with his stripes we are healed." (Isa. 53:5)

I'm sure by now you see clearly what I was doing with the material I inherited and what others before me had been doing. We were redefining "Messiahship" in terms of suffering unto death. We were convinced, we had heard, and we had experienced that deliverance *that way* was by far more profound, more promising, and more pervasive than mere military-political liberation from socio-economic oppression and enslavement, or even some mindboggling spectacular, other-worldly "salvation" event. In any case we were convinced, and we believed there was convincing support in the divinely ordered history and the divinely inspired prophetic words of our forebears that Jesus, as God's agent, had accomplished this, God's will, in this God's way.

But I must soon bring this discourse to a close. I am going to comment briefly on the other places where this theme appears, sketch two other themes, point out some of my connections, introductions, and summaries, give you an outline and leave it there in your hands.

You have already been signaled that I am defining Messiahship (Christ) and the role of "the Son of God" in terms of suffering unto death (1:11). Did you feel the tension begin with Jesus' temptation (1:12–13), increase with the arrest of John the Baptist (1:14), intensify further when Jesus is confronted by "a man with an unclean spirit" (1:23) and when the scribes questioned "in their hearts" ("'Why does this man speak thus? It is blasphemy! Who can forgive sins but God alone?'" 2:7)? Blasphemy is a deadly serious charge.

An atmosphere of foreboding is gathering. It increases when the scribes of the Pharisees criticize Jesus for eating with "'tax collectors and sinners.'" (2:16) We've only read one and a half chapters and Jesus is already in trouble! We can feel it, can't we? We know what often happens to people who engage in direct action and break the social rules that are sanctioned by religion and equated with divine law. It's happened in your recent history. Then that little somber note is struck in the middle of the discussion about fasting: " 'The days will come, when the bridegroom is taken away from them, and then they will fast in that day.' " (2:20) A joyful occasion: a wedding celebration. The bridegroom is present. The wedding guests feast. The bridegroom is taken away. They fast. Like the sad sighing of a breeze through the trees, as a dark cloud passes overhead, signaling a distant but approaching storm, while gay music is played, glasses tinkle, happy voices and laughter sound forth during an afternoon garden party.

Then, in case there was any doubt about what to expect, the situation is clarified in 2:23–3:6. Controversy over keeping or breaking sabbath law is climaxed with "The Pharisees went out, and immediately held counsel with the Herodians against him, how to destroy him." (3:6) The religious leaders, guardians of the mores and the morals, seek the assistance of the thoroughly secular, socio-economic and political pragmatists, in opposition to Jesus. They're out to get him. Does he stand a chance?

Some scribes from Jerusalem absurdly charge him with being in league with the devil (3:22)! His friends fear that he's crazy (3:21). Neither of these implications will increase his personal safety or his social security. In the explanation of the parable of the sower (which probably originated in the believing community after Jesus' death–resurrection) a seed of dramatic anticipation is sown (which by the time I put this passage in had already borne a bitter harvest): " 'Then, when tribulation or persecution arises on account of the word, immediately they fall away.' " (4:17) The story of the death of John the Baptist (6:14–29) is also a forewarning and a foreshadowing. If it happened to the forerunner, what else can we expect for the runner? After all, their messages were much the same (cf. 1:4 and 1:14).

In the preface to the story of "The Feeding of the Five Thousand" I make an allusion to "sheep without a shepherd" (6:34) and then again, after Jesus' last meal with his disciples, just before his betrayal and crucifixion, I include a similar reference: "And Jesus said to them, 'You will all fall away; for it is written, "I will strike the shepherd, and the sheep will be scattered." ' " (14:27) Readers or hearers familiar with their

Old Testament (especially the Greek version, which is the one from which I quoted)[30] would have recognized the source of these two allusions as the book of the prophet Zechariah (see especially Zech. 10:4 and 13:7). They would have known that the oracles in this scroll were partly about faithlessness, judgment, suffering, distress, bad shepherds, death, and a good shepherd rejected by his sheep (Zech. 10:1–3; 11:1–17; 13:7). They would have known that Zechariah also prophesies salvation, restoration, a gathering of a (remnant) faithful flock on the other side of judgment, suffering, distress, and death (e.g., 9:1–17; 10:3*b*–12).[31]

Many of your scholars have noticed that the approximate mid-point in my Gospel (8:27–33) is also the crucial turning point. Immediately after Peter confesses Jesus to be the Christ, Jesus begins to teach the disciples "that the Son of man must suffer many things, and be rejected by the elders and the chief priests and the scribes, and be killed, and after three days rise again. And he said this plainly." (8:31–32*a*) Notice the *must*. What is happening and is about to happen is not accidental; nor is it merely humanly volitional (by the will of man). With Jesus acting and speaking as he does, within the human socio-economic, cultural-political-religious context, it certainly seems plausible that he would be rejected and killed. However, the emphasis is on God's intention. God is the director of this eschatological drama, this soteriological scenario, this purposive passion play. It is *his* will. Anyone, even a disciple, who cannot comprehend this, who refuses to accept this, who resists this or denies this is acting and speaking like Satan, the Tempter from the will and the way of God (1:13), and the "father of lies." (John 8:44; Acts 5:3)

The remainder of the passsages I've listed, the warp-and-weft interlacings of this bold red design so prominently woven into the fabric of my Gospel tapestry, simply repeat, demonstrate, and develop this theme unto its climactic conclusion in 15:39.

Jesus' prediction of the suffering, death, and resurrection of "the Son of man" is repeated twice after 8:31 (9:30–32; 10:33–34). On two other occasions (9:33–34; 10:35–41), after Peter's rebuke of Jesus when Jesus insists that "the Son of man" must suffer (8:31–33), the disciples of Jesus display that they do not understand or make the definitive connection between the identity-mission of Jesus and his suffering unto death. As I purposefully portray the story, immediately after Jesus (again) teaches the disciples that " 'the Son of man will be delivered into the hands of men, and they will kill him; and when he is killed, after three days he will rise,' " (9:31) on the way to Capernaum they start discussing who is "the greatest"! (9:33–34) They can't seem to get the point until the whole passion play is performed. The way I put my scenes together the disciples apparently didn't even really hear Jesus when he told them (back in 8:34ff.) that if any person would come after him he or she must deny the self, " 'take up' " the cross and follow him. " 'For whoever would save his life will lose it; and whoever loses his life for my sake and the gospel's will save it.' " How could the disciples have been discussing who was "the greatest"? Not only had they not gotten the message about Jesus' suffering, they also had not assimilated the fact that that is the way the disciple goes too. Jesus tries to educate them (e.g., 8:34–9:1; 9:35–37; 10:42–45), but they are slow to learn. In fact they *never* learn (e.g., 10:38–45; 14:3–9, 27–31, 32–42, 47, 49–50, 60–72; 16:1–8). When he was arrested "they all forsook him, and fled." (14:50) Many women watched at his crucifixion, but apparently none of his male disciples were present (15:40f.). None of his (male) disciples came with the women to the tomb (16:1). Apparently they had all gone back (disappointed?) to Galilee. Or did they learn between Jesus' crucifixion and their reunion with him in Galilee, after his resurrection (cf. 14:28 and 16:7); or did they not learn until they experienced him alive in their midst back home? You may wish to ponder these questions further, but I must return to this third instance of disciple obtuseness. "In 10:35–41 it is James and John who ask for places of power in the kingdom, apparently not realizing that Jesus' glory cannot occur before he dies."[32] And again Jesus attempts to teach them the truth of this theme of salvation and suffering (10:42–45).

Was it a historical fact that the disciples of Jesus were so dense? Probably not. As you read the story, Jesus speaks "plainly" (8:32*a*; 4:33–34; cf. 9:30–32; 10:33–34). According to my presentation of the drama they also had a great deal of supportive evidence that Jesus was God's agent before his death (e.g., exorcisms, acknowledgments by demons, healings, miracles, testimonies from believers, even the transfiguration 9:2–8)! Was I, then, for some strange reason trying to make the Lord's first followers look dull and cowardly? No. Did I have some antagonism or bias against Peter and some of his followers contemporary with me which I was insinuating in my document? No. As I have mentioned before, I was telling my story freely, creatively, in such a way as to indicate clearly that no one (not even a disciple) can rightly and adequately understand the meaning of any part prior to the end, without knowing the conclusion (15) and the continuation (16), in other words, the very meaning of this theme.

I will not comment further on the other passages. I believe their meanings within this motif will now be self-evident. That the suffering and death of God's agent are essential in the divine drama of salvation is made evident in numerous places following the "must" of 8:31. For example, in Jesus' "rebuke" of Peter: " 'Get behind me, Satan! For you are not on the side of God, but of man.' " (8:33); in the "it is written" of 9:12; 14:21 and 27; and in the "let the scriptures be fulfilled" in 14:49. In fact, as all readers and hearers of my Gospel familiar with the Hebrew-Jewish scriptures will readily recognize I present my entire passion play, and particularly the last act (*denouement, finale,* and *continuum* or *epilogue,* 14–16) as fulfillment of the previously declared and enacted "word of God," as I and those of my community interpreted it.

Before I finally conclude my discussion of this theme, however, I want to call your attention to a couple of structural patterns that appear within it. (1) Did you notice that the title "Son of God" used for Jesus was placed in three prominent places and defined in each in terms of suffering? At the beginning of my Gospel (1:1 plus 1:11); at the middle, within the story of "The Transfiguration" (9:7; recall my previous comments on this story: it is immediately followed by Jesus' instruction that, as it was written, "the Son of man should suffer many things..." 9:12); and at the end, in the mouth of the centurian, as Jesus is hanging dead on the cross (15:39).[33] (This title is also alluded to in "The Parable of the Vineyard," a story of rejection, death, and judgment [12:6], and it is spoken by unclean spirits [3:11; 5:7; cf. 1:24].[34] (2) Was it obvious that a three-fold pattern was being repeated three times in chapters 8–10?[35] The predictions of suffering, death, and resurrection (8:31; 9:30–32; 10:33–34); the lack of understanding on the part of the disciples (8:32–33;

9:33–34; 10:35–41); Jesus' teaching on the "nature of discipleship" (8:34–38; 9:35–37; 10:42–45).
Professor Achtemeier sees "a fourth element in the pattern."

> It is a tradition in which Jesus is shown to be different from, or have powers beyond those of, ordinary men. In 9:2–8 it is the story of the transfiguration; in 9:38–41 it is a discussion of the power of Jesus' name which allows others by its use to cast out demons; in 10:46–52 it is the story of the healing of blind Bartimaeus. Are these traditions also meant by Mark to be part of the recurring pattern? If so, what point do they make in the pattern? If not, why are they included in each instance at the end of the pattern?[36]

Is it possible that they each suggest in their own way what has been signaled by the previous combination of three: that contrary to what people normally think, the different, extraordinary, and powerful are by God manifest in the apparently familiar, ordinary, and weak?

Christology

At various places within what I have said thus far and within my Gospel you will have noticed I referred to Jesus by certain specific titles; these titles are telling. For example, (the) Christ, Son of David, Prophet, Lord, Teacher, Son of God, Son of man. All of these titles were originally used by Christians in various places to symbolize and signify their understanding of the profound and ultimate meaning of this Jew, Jesus of Nazareth (1:9; 1:24). These titles were all present in the sources which I used. They each, therefore, brought a history of accumulated interpretive significance which, it was believed, contributed to the total meaning of Jesus and his story for the lives of individuals and groups. I will, briefly, discuss possible and probable connotations of each of these titles. I will concentrate on the last one, "Son of man," since that was the one I preferred,[37] the one I thought most effectively conveyed the essential meaning of Jesus. It was necessary for me to redefine, or give a particular modified meaning to each of these titles, including "Son of man," in order to communicate my particular conception of how Jesus functioned as the authoritative agent of God, the decisive act of God. In the Hebrew language this representative agent of God is called "the anointed One" (e.g., 1 Sam. 16:6; 24:6), *ha Mashiach*, the Messiah, the chosen, designated ambassador of God commissioned to speak and act on God's behalf within human history, specifically as the Deliverer of his people, the Jews, from his enemies and their oppressors. Translated from Hebrew into Greek *ha Mashiach,* the Messiah, becomes *ho Christos,* "The Christ." From this word we get "Christology" which is the explication of the meaning of Jesus as "the Christ," the God-appointed "savior." This little historical word study has already taken us into our first title for Jesus, i.e., "Christ."

Christ

By the time I wrote my Gospel, the title "Christ" in my sources and generally among Christians, had already become the second part of a double name designation for this Jew, Jesus of Nazareth: Jesus Christ (1:1).³⁸ For most non-Jewish Christians it had no startling significance. For Jewish Christians, *when applied to Jesus,* if it was more than a name, it certainly underwent some radical modification of meaning! The dominant traditional Jewish understanding of "the Messiah" was that of a God-anointed, royal, humanly powerful, politico-military deliverer. Obviously, if Jesus was "the Christ" he was a different kind, and his deliverance was of a different order. This is precisely what my sources and the Christians who produced them professed and proclaimed. The mode and manner of Jesus' being "the Christ" was that of suffering unto crucifixion and resurrection, with the result being deliverance from the old deadly existence to the new lively reality of "now and forever." (E.g., 10:29–31) This was the accumulated/interpretive significance of this title as I received it. I let it stand thus in the sources which I employed within my Gospel in the following places: 1:1; 8:29 (cf. 30–31); 9:41; 12:35–37 (a debate over Messianic lineage suggesting that it was not necessary for the Messiah to be a genealogical descendant of David); 13:21–22; 14:61; 15:32 (cf. 15:2, 9, 12, 18). Please do not miss the ironic *double entendre* which occurs in the application of this title (plus "King of the Jews") to the humiliated, suffering, and dying Jesus of "The Passion Narrative" (14:61; 15:32; cf. 15:2, 9, 12, 18). Within this context "Jesus Christ, the King of the Jews" takes on a new meaning. What a king! And what a kingdom (1:15; 4:26, 30; 9:1; 10:15, 23f.; 11:10; 12:34; 15:43)! The sovereign, authoritative rule of God within history and beyond history is essentially characterized by the reign of this representative vice-regent enthroned on a cross (15:25–26).

Son of David

Since I was writing, as I have said, primarily for Christians outside of Palestine, outside the erstwhile nation-state-kingdom of Israel (it had not existed for generations and was never to exist again until your modern era), and since this title reflected those futile and fanatical hopes for a divine-human restoration of this kind of kingdom (political power and program), I had little interest in or use for the title "Son of David." Where it occurred in my sources I allowed it to remain. I did not expurgate it but, again, within the context of my dramatic interpretation of Jesus I redefined it (10:47, 48; 11:1-11).

Prophet

The title "prophet," though certainly appropriate for Jesus (he spoke and enacted the word and will of God, called people to repentance and entrance into "the kingdom of God," e.g., 1:15) was not a terribly important definition of Jesus for me. It also was present in some of my sources (6:4; 6:15; 8:28). I did not remove it, but neither did I play upon it. In the story of Jesus' teaching in the synagogue and his subsequent rejection at Nazareth it appears that he implied this title for himself. In all the other instances where it occurs in my Gospel it is spoken as a penultimate misunderstanding of Jesus' identity, one person short of who he really is (6:15; 8:28). He was not the prophetic-announcer or forerunner of the One; he *was* (is) the One!

Lord

I'm certain you are familiar with the use of the title "Lord" for Jesus. This usage was widespread in the Gentile-Christian churches. Among these non-Jewish Greek-speaking brothers and sisters this title formed a part of their earliest, simplest, and most complete confession of faith. In Greek it was "Iesus Kurios," "Jesus (is) Lord." In this form (with the word order reversed in the Greek text for emphasis) Paul quotes it at the conclusion of an early Christian hymn of praise in his letter to the Philippians (Phil. 2:11).

In the third century B.C., when the Jews who had been dispersed from their homeland and had been living in Egypt for generations forgot how to speak and read Hebrew and therefore needed a translation of their scriptures into the common language of their day and their world, the scribes who made the translation chose the Greek word *kurios* to translate the unique Hebrew-Jewish name for God (*Yahweh*,

Exod. 3:13–15). So you can see that for some Jews and Christians this title could be quite loaded with sacred significance. Jews, generally, would have considered it blasphemy, a religious offense punishable by stoning to death (cf. Mark 14:64 where Jesus is falsely charged with this crime), to call any human being *kurios* meaning God (Yahweh). Other religions of the Greco-Roman world claimed "many 'gods' and many 'lords'" (1 Cor. 8:5)–but not Judaism. The word *kurios* (lord) could also be used simply as a human title of respect (sir), or not only to signify human respect but also to recognize human authority (Lord or master), as "the Lord and Master" over a household. In certain situations *kurios* was also employed to acknowledge *ultimate* authority, human or otherwise. Early in the first century A.D. a test of loyalty to the Roman state as the citizen's supreme authority, and Caesar as the ultimate authority within the state, was put in the form of a loyalty oath, *Kurios Kaisar* ("[the] Lord is Caesar" or "Caesar is Lord"). In the minds of many people (and sometimes in official imperial pronouncements) "Lord" in this title signified not only divine designation, but also divine person and power. Refusal to take this oath or pledge of allegiance to Caesar as "Lord" could result in punishment by death (by crucifixion or by being devoured alive by wild beasts in the arena). It was a choice many first century Christians had to make.

The Greek word *kurios* occurs fourteen times in my Gospel (1:3; 2:28; 5:19; 7:28; 11:3, 9; 12:9; 11, 29, 30, 36 [twice], 37; 13:20). Of these fourteen occurrences seven appear in quotations from the Old Testament (1:3 in Isaiah 40:3; 11:9 in Psalm 118:26; 12:11 in Psalm 118:23; 12:29, 30 in Deut. 6:4; 12:36 in Psalm 110:1 [two occurrences]). Of these seven quotations five are clearly references to *Yahweh*, God of the Hebrews (11:9; 12:11, 29, 30, 36 first usage). One appearance of *kurios* in an Old Testament quotation is a reference to an Israelite king (12:36, second usage, "my Lord," from Psalm 110:1). In the passage in my Gospel where this quotation occurs Jesus is arguing against a teaching of "the scribes" that the expected Messiah must come from the royal lineage of David. In 1:3 (Isaiah 40:3) the use of the Old Testament quotation suggests that Jesus is, in a sense which my whole Gospel will define, the fulfillment of the ancient prophecy of the coming Lord whose "way" is to be "prepared." Of the remaining seven uses of *kurios* in my Gospel three more are clearly not references to Jesus. In 12:9 *kurios* refers to "the owner of the vineyard"; in 12:37 to the Messiah; in 13:20 to God.

As for the remaining four occurrences of *kurios* in my Gospel we may note the following: In 2:28 it appears in a "saying" of Jesus, " 'The sabbath was made for man, not man for the sabbath; so the Son of man is lord even of the sabbath.' " In this instance the meaning of *kurios* may be simply "master." In the story of Jesus' healing of "the Gerasene demoniac," the healed man is told by Jesus, " 'Go home to your friends, and tell them how much the Lord has done for you, and how he has had mercy on you.' " (5:19) Although in your Revised Standard English version the word Lord is capitalized here, in my original Greek text the word *kurios* was not. In fact the word kurios was nowhere capitalized in my Greek sources. Therefore, in this case also, the meaning may simply be "master." These observations apply also to 7:28 where the Syrophoenician woman is addressing Jesus (" 'Yes, Lord; yet even the dogs under the table eat the children's crumbs' ") and 11:3 where Jesus is addressing his disciples telling them to go into Jerusalem to borrow a "colt" for his use (" 'If anyone says to you, "Why are you doing this?" say, "The Lord has need of it and will send it back immediately" ' "). The meaning of the title "Lord" in these four verses (as well as in 1:3) may be somewhat ambivalent. However it is important to remember that these stories about Jesus were preserved and used in communities of believers who professed with deep conviction and profound meaning: *'Iesus Christos Kurios,* Jesus Christ is Lord!

"Teacher" is one of my two preferred titles for Jesus. (The other, my first preference, is "Son of man.") I use it numerous times in my document (e.g., 4:38; 9:17, 38; 10:17, 35; 12:14, 19, 32; 13:1; 14:14, by Jesus with reference to himself; cf. 10:51 and 11:21 where the word Rabbi occurs). As teacher Jesus was a teller of parables about the kingdom (authoritative rule) of God (e.g., 3:23–27), its reception or rejection (4:1–9), its hidden and nonspectacular but nonetheless real and powerful presence (4:30–32), and its inevitable and imminent realization (4:26–29). As "teacher" he enacted this divine authority and power as he cast out demons (e.g.,

Teacher

1:21–28), healed the sick (e.g., 9:14–27; cf. 10:46–52), and stilled the storm (4:35–41). As "teacher" he debated authoritatively with the religious leaders (12:13–37) and "cleansed the temple" (11:15–19), thereby removing religion from any equation with code or cult. As "teacher" he gave instruction for the inheritance of "eternal life" (10:17–22) and about the appropriate life-style of a disciple between the present and the fast approaching consummation of his mission (13). Most definitively as "teacher" he taught his disciples that "the Son of man must suffer" (e.g., 8:31; 9:31) and that they must follow (8:34–9:1). Jesus refers to himself as "teacher" when he instructs two of his disciples to secure a guest room in Jerusalem in which they may eat their last and symbolic supper together (14:13f.). This motif of Jesus as Teacher will be discussed further when I tell you about some of the literary devices which I used in composing my Gospel (i.e., interpretive connections).

Son of God   I have made brief explanatory and interpretive references to my use of the title "Son of God" in my discussion of the previous theme, "Suffering unto Salvation"; and I will explore its significance again briefly in my forthcoming description of some of the theological-literary-structural characteristics of my Gospel. Therefore, I will not go into an extended discussion of its possible and probable meanings now. I will simply remind you that rather than a divine godman which many Greeks and Romans worshipped, the term denoted to Jews either an individual (e.g., Ps. 2:7) or a corporate (e.g., "Israel," Exod. 4:22) human representative and active agent chosen, sent, and empowered by God to speak God's word and to do God's will. Actually, the title of my document (1:1) suggests that I am defining my understanding of Jesus as "Son of God" by the way I employ this reference to him in my proclamation about him. The reader/hearer will come to know what I mean by "Son of God" in my Gospel as he or she encounters this designation of Jesus and ponders its significance within each context where it occurs. Furthermore, what I mean by "Son of God" is finally the total portrait of Jesus which I present in my whole document, start to finish. In order to understand the meaning of Jesus as "Son of God" one must experience this person, his story and its meaning all the way through (even into the present which is the current continuation of this "gospel of Jesus Christ, the Son of God" [1:1]). (See also 16:1–8.) With this approach to the text in mind read the following passages asking yourself how Jesus is *functioning* as "Son of God" or what *characteristics* of the "Son of God" are being displayed: 1:9–11; 3:7–12; 5:1–13; 9:2–13; 13:32–37; 14:53–65; 15:33–39.

"Son of man" is my favorite, special title for Jesus, the one through which I personally most completely understand him, interpret him, and portray him. I got this title first from the apocalyptic-eschatological book of Daniel in the Old Testament. This is a highly symbolic document written about 165 B.C. during a time of persecution, suffering, and severe distress for the Jewish people under the Greek rulers. The six stories and four dream-visions within this book read as if they had their historical setting within the Babylonian captivity of the Jews under King Nebuchadnezzar in the sixth century B.C. By means of this back-dating, the author of this book disguised the meaning of its contents and hid them from those who could not understand, namely the oppressive Greek rulers. This book is called apocalyptic (from apocalypse, meaning a disclosure, or a revelation, from the Greek verb which signifies a drawing back of a curtain, or an unveiling) because it claims to reveal that side to this side, the supra-historical to the historical, the divine side to the human side, and the future to the present. It is called eschatological because its message is about the end of the present age and the beginning of the New Age. I think I can do no better here than ask Professor Achtemeier to summarize the results of his study of this title.

Son of Man

> In Dan. 7:13, the phrase, highly qualified, is used to describe the central figure in Daniel's fifth night-vision who ultimately receives dominion over all the peoples of the earth. This figure is interpreted as the "saints of the Most High" in v. 18, thus making it represent the faithful remnant of Israel. The title also occurs in later apocryphal writings. In 1 Enoch it designates a figure who in the last times will judge and overthrow the wicked and uphold the righteous (chaps. 46–53), and he is also called the "Anointed one" and the "Elect one," thus clearly designating him as eschatological deliverer of Israel. In 4 Ezra a similar eschatological avenger is described, but his title is simply "Man," although it may belong to the "Son of man" tradition.

The extent to which this title represented a firm set of eschatological expectations in the time of Jesus has been much debated, as has the question whether or not an actual figure designated with the title "Son of man" was expected to appear in the last times. It is very difficult, therefore, to come to any firm conclusion about what expectations the Jews of Jesus' time associated with this title, if indeed it was a familiar eschatological title to them at all. In one passage in Mark which Mark appears to have assembled from his traditions, Jesus seems to be referring to the Son of man as someone different from himself (8:38). If, however, Jesus ever did speak of a Son of man as someone different from himself, by the time Mark wrote his Gospel, that title had been firmly attached to Jesus.

Whatever conclusion we may want to reach on the pre-Christian expectations attached to the title "Son of man," it is clear that Mark feels this title is the one most adequate to express the meaning of Jesus of Nazareth. It can be used to designate Jesus during his earthly career. At the very beginning of his account of Jesus' activity, Mark places two traditions in which that title refers to Jesus as he carried on his ministry in Galilee (2:1–12; 2:27–28). The title can also be used to refer to Jesus as the one who was betrayed (14:21), arrested (14:41), who died (10:45), who was raised from the dead (9:9), who was seated at God's right hand in heaven (14:62), and who would come at the end of the age to gather the faithful into God's kingdom (13:26).

It is obvious that Mark can use this designation to correct the more familiar christological titles that also appeared in the traditions he had at his disposal, but which were open to ambiguous understanding. When Peter confesses that Jesus is the Christ, Jesus responds with a statement of the impending fate of the Son of man, thus implicitly correcting the former title by the latter one (8:29–31). The same holds true of the trial scene. There, when the high priest combines the two familiar christological titles in his question to Jesus, Jesus acknowledges the applicability of those titles to himself, but then corrects them by referring to himself as the Son of man (14:61–62). A further indication of the importance of this title for Mark's christological understanding of Jesus lies in the fact that Jesus is the only one in the whole of the Gospel who uses this title. Mark presents this one christological designation as the favorite title of Jesus for himself. Not only does this make clear its unambiguous nature, so far as Mark is concerned, but it also, again so far as Mark is concerned, was capable of expressing Jesus' own self-understanding. This self-understanding, implied in most of the passages where the title Son of man is used, is perhaps best expressed when Jesus speaks of himself as one who serves, and who will die for others (10:45).

It is in fact this understanding of Jesus as one who must suffer, die, and who will rise, that represents the controlling christological emphasis in Mark's Gospel. If Jesus is the key to the Gospel narrative, then Jesus as suffering Son of man gives us the clue to unravel many of the mysteries that present themselves to the reader of that narrative.[39]

Eschatology

As I have remarked already in several contexts, and will undoubtedly mention again, one of my main concerns was to clear up any misconceptions about the future return of Jesus (the *parousia*) on the one hand, and on the other to emphasize that he was, indeed, coming back finally to conclude this unfinished drama. I am aware that my multiple endings and beginnings can get confusing. So let me try to clarify: with the appearance of Jesus on the stage of human history (1:9–11 and 1:14f.), through his person, words, and deeds the end (*eschaton*) of the "old age" is signaled ("the time is fulfilled, and the kingdom of God is at hand," 1:15). The era of the relative reign of evil, sin, bondage, and death is ended (e.g., 1:24, 34; 3:23–27; 2:1–12; 5:35–43; 12). The beginning of the "new age" of goodness, forgiveness, freedom, and life has arrived (e.g., 1:21–2:12; 2:23–3:6; 5:35–43; 6:30–44; 7:31–37; 8:1–10; 9:35; *10:29; 12:28–34). The "old age" forces desperately resist the inbreaking of the power of God through his "Son" and agent, Jesus, "the Son of man" (e.g., 1:24; 3:6, 27, 28–30; 7:5–13; 8:31–33; 9:30–32; 10:32–34; 12:1–12; 14:43–15:39). In their frantic resistance against him they kill him (14:43–15:39). This is another ending. The curtain comes down on what we interpreted to be both the ending of the last act of the old play and the first act of the new play. Obviously there is an overlap here.

Then there is a *new beginning*: The resurrection of Jesus (16:1–8). This experience signals the beginning of the final (eternal) conclusion (the actual realization in history of the suprahistorical [transcendent] kingdom of God [the "New Age"] in totality. It also signals the end of that previous overlap period during which the conflict between the two ages was joined. Now there is a short interim period characterized both by resurrection (life) and crucifixion (death). The experience of the resurrection of Jesus has signified and confirmed to the faithful which of these is ultimately superior and definitive, even in the present. But *this present* will be *ended* also when Jesus returns to establish finally and completely the realm of life.

Now this is where chapters 13 and 16 come into focus. They are the ones I used to really communicate the elements of this situation. Paul Achtemeier, Professor of New Testament at Union Theological Seminary in Virginia, has done such an excellent job of summarizing in some detail what I did in and with these chapters, I'm going to suggest that you read what he has to say on the subject.[40]

If you will read chapter 13 attentively, I think you will notice that it breaks down into three sections: 13:1–5a (Introduction); 13:5b–31 (Main Middle section); 13:32–37 (Conclusion). Most of the material in this chapter was circulating around Christian communities in regions of the Roman Empire like my own as a separate document before I got a copy of it. Originally it was a Jewish or Jewish Christian apocalyptic pamphlet stating that events then underway signaled the beginning of the end of this (interim) period of human history. Reading this pamphlet gave some of my Christian brothers and sisters ideas. Some of them I agreed with and some of them I didn't. So I took this pamphlet, gave it an introduction (13:1–5a) and edited it, correcting its misleading ideas and communicating those which I believed to be right, by inserting some of my own.

The main problems with the pamplet as I got it were two: (1) it was trying to ascertain and predict exactly when the end (the eschaton), which we Christians believed would be the return of Christ (the parousia), would occur (13:4); and (2) it was saying that this had already happened (vss. 6, 21–22), or, at least that it was beginning to happen *right now*; that then-current events were signs of its occurrence (e.g., vss. 7a, 8a, b, 9, 11a, 12, 14–30, 28–31). I disagreed with both these ideas. I believed that, as Christians, we should not try to predict exactly when the parousia would occur (vss. 32–37). This kind of prediction about the unkown can lead only to confusion and anxiety. Already there were some people who were afraid that the parousia had already happened and they had missed it (vss. 5a, 6, 21–23, cf. 2 Thess. 2:1–5).[41] One thing I wanted to do in chapter 13 was to assure my readers and hearers that this was not true (vss. 5*b*, 7, 21–23) and that when the Lord did in fact return "the attendant signs" would "be of such character that no one could possible miss seeing them (vss. 24–26) and no follower of Jesus could possibly miss being included in it (vs. 27)."[42] The attempt to predict the final end (and the *new* new beginning of eternal life—more a super-good *quality* than a never-ending *quantity*, in our Jewish minds) was not only unhelpful (confusing, misleading, and anxiety-producing) it was also unfaithful. It was (and is) tantamount to the attempt to control tightly the present by precisely predicting the future, and thereby to control or manipulate God. That is neither possible nor proper. Rather the appropriate posture for the Christian is one of alert trust, watching faithfulness, expectant and confident commitment (vss. 32–37; cf. vss. 5, 9, 23).

Although I strongly disagreed with the rumor that the final end-beginning time was already upon us and the attempt to predict precisely when the parousia would occur, I did agree that it was unquestionably coming and that it was very near (cf. 9:1; 13:30; 14:25). That's partly why I "picked up on" and revised this pamphlet in the first place and gave it prominence and a key position in my Gospel (between the disclosive-definitive actions and teachings of Jesus, beginning with the entry into Jerusalem [11:1–11], and the final revelatory events of his last supper, crucifixion, and resurrection [14–16]). I wanted to warn my readers "against premature claims that the end is imminent (vs. 7*b*, 8*c*, 10, 23*b*)," but I also wanted "to warn them that the end is nonetheless coming soon, and they had better be about the business of watching for it (vss. 30, 33, 35–37)."[43] It will undoubtedly be preceded by suffering (13:8–13). But just as surely those who endure "to the end will be saved." (13:13)

As you will surely notice, my Gospel ends rather abruptly: "And they [the women] went out and fled from the tomb; for trembling and astonishment had come upon them; and they said nothing to any one, for they were afraid." (16:8) Actually, the word order in the Greek text stops with the preposition "for" (*gar* in Greek). This is unusual grammar. But, as I will discuss further, it implies an "unfinishedness," a "continuedness." It points to the future, this same eschatological future which chapter 13 proclaims. Professor Achtemeier has expressed my feeling-meaning well.

> The resurrection is announced and the reaction is one of ambiguity. The women "feared." The key to understanding who Jesus is has now been provided, as Mark has indicated all through his narrative it would be: with the resurrection, following the suffering, it will be possible to understand who Jesus really is. The resurrection has now occurred, Jesus can now be understood truly for what he is (the fact that Mark would write and that the gospel could be preached demonstrate that fact), and yet fear—and mystery—remain.
>
> The risen Jesus is still the same Jesus as he was in Nazareth: he remains obscured by the events in which he participates. He taught and worked his acts of power in Galilee, and he yet remained obscure in his real identity and true meaning. He has risen, and yet he remains obscured by the events that continue to occur in the world: war, famine, persecution, false claims (as outlined in chapter 13). Only with his return in visible glory will that mystery finally be eliminated, will that obscurity finally vanish. Then even his enemies will have to recognize him for what he is (14:62); then the cosmos itself will announce his coming in signs no one can miss (13:24–25); then those who have remained faithful will experience the deliverance for which they have yearned (4:20; 13:13b). Yet until that time, mystery remains drawn over Jesus, now risen. The Jesus who drew rejection because of the ambiguity of his first appearance on earth continues in that same ambiguous way now as risen and powerful Lord. Only the final events will, once and for all, remove such ambiguity.
>
> Therefore, the word for the readers of Mark's Gospel is: watch (13:37). Ambiguity remains: the women's reaction to the news that Christ has risen from the dead was—fear. Suffering remains: before Christ returns in his risen power, Christians will undergo unparalleled suffering in the course of the lives they lead as followers of their crucified and risen Lord. The possibility of rejecting Jesus remains: the world continues to throw barriers in the path of faithful discipleship in the form of "delight in riches, and the desires for other things" (4:19). Only at the end does the grain ripen for harvest. Only at the end does the mustard seed produce the tree. The word remains, therefore: watch![44]

This eschatological outlook characterized the community in which I lived and in which I composed my Gospel. This apocalyptic perspective defined the mode of being for those Christians among whom and, in part, for whom I fashioned my proclamation. Therefore, it is not surprising that my document took the form of an apocalyptic (disclosing that side or the new age to this side in the old age) eschatological (end-time) drama.

It is not essential to know whether I (we) lived in or near Rome (the traditional answer) or in Syria, as Professor Howard Clark Kee argues in his recent responsible, careful, and detailed study of my Gospel, *Community of the New Age: Studies in Mark's Gospel*[45] or some other place in the Roman Empire of the first century. In any case I (we) got around (e.g., 6:7–12; 7:24–30). Yes, some of us were spirit-filled (charismatic) prophets, preachers, and healers. But whatever our names, origins, and vocations, our common and definitive outlook was apocalyptic-eschatological—looking forward to the final and full disclosure—actualization of that kingdom (that other mode of being) which Jesus announced and enacted.

Now let us consider briefly some of the intentional editorial devices which I used in order to further communicate my Gospel meaning.

Many of your scholars have long observed that I had certain special ways of connecting (and thus shaping) the material which I used in composing my Gospel. The way they discovered that these connective words and introductory phrases (or whole sentences) originated with me was by noticing that Matthew and Luke sometimes did not use these same ones, and that when one didn't, the other one often did. — Theological Editorial Techniques

Interpretive Connections

Practically all of the content of my Gospel is found either in Matthew or Luke, or both. (The only major omissions are 3:19*b*–21; 4:26–29; 7:31–37; 8:22–26; 9:49f. [cf. Matt. 5:13; Luke 14:34f.] and 14:51–52.) Both Matthew and Luke usually follow my order (and to a great degree my exact wording). Whenever one of them deviates from my order of material the other normally stays with me. They almost never agree with each other against the order I constructed. It was observations like these that led your scholars to discover the most widely accepted current solution to the synoptic problem, i.e., how the Gospels bearing the names of Matthew, — *The Synoptic Problem*

Mark, and Luke are chonologically and literarily related. This was one of the main questions literary criticism was seeking to answer. It was called the synoptic problem, as most of you know, because in a synopsis of the contents of these three Gospels given side by side, in parallel columns, one can see the close similarities, as well as the important differences among them. Also, as the two Greek words which form the English word "synopsis" (*syn* meaning "with" or "together" and "*opsis*" like "optic" meaning "sight" or "view") suggest, they can be "seen together." This also is why each one of them is called a Synoptic Gospel. A quick comparison between these three and the Gospel of John will show why John is not called a Synoptic Gospel. It is quite different from these three in content, wording, and order.

The current solution to the synoptic problem says that I wrote my Gospel first, that both Matthew and Luke used my document as a source for writing theirs, plus another common source, designated "Q" from the first letter of the German word for "source," "Quelle," and special material that each got within their respective communities. Each of them wrote their Gospels at different times and at different places within different communities, with their own particular motives, concerns, ideas, and purposes in mind. Many of your scholars suggest that Matthew was written primarily for Greek-speaking Jewish Christians in the area of Syria, sometime between 75 and 85 A.D., and that Luke (plus Acts) was composed between 70 and 90 A.D. by a non-Jewish Christian for Gentile Christians somewhere (Caesarea, Greece, Rome are three possibilities) in the Roman Empire. For the details of all this see the summaries presented in Professor Kümmel's *Introduction to the New Testament* (pp. 33–106) or Professors Kee, Young, and Froelich, *Understanding the New Testament,* 3rd edition, pp. 74–93.

Linguistic Editorial Devices

Now please allow me simply and briefly to give summary descriptions of four interpretive connections (linguistic editorial devices) which I used and indicate the meanings I wished to convey through them.

My intention in frequently using the words *euthus* and *eutheos* meaning "immediately" or "at once" as short connections or transitions was to create and communicate a heightened sense of urgency, quickness, or immediacy. I wanted the reader to feel the urgent, immediate character of the action of God through Jesus in both the past and the present (especially in, with, and through the activity of our community of the faithful). I also wanted the reader to know of the imminent return of Jesus to complete his divine mission and consummate God's authoritative rule (over the whole universe and all of human history and especially, benevolently, within our new community of the faithful). I use one or the other of these words at the following junctures in my Gospel: *Euthus*: 1:12, 28; 1:3; *Eutheos*: 1:31, 42; 2:8, 12; 4:5, 15, 16, 17, 29; 5:2, 30; 6:27, 50; 10:52; 14:43; 1:10, 18, 20, 21; 2:2; 3:6; 5:29, 42; 6:25, 45, 54; 7:35; 8:10; 9:15, 20, 24; 11:3; 14:45; 15:1; 1:29, 43; 5:13; 1:30; 5:36; 11:2.[46] This sense of urgency and feeling of directness are reflected also in my use of "harsh" or "abrupt" words such as "split" (1:10) and "thrown out." (1:12)[47] "And when he [Jesus] came up out of the water, immediately [*euthus*] he saw the heavens opened [or "split," Greek *schidzomenous*] and the Spirit descending upon him like a dove.... The Spirit immediately [*euthus*] drove ["threw," or "cast out," literally "is casting out" or "throwing out," Greek *ekballei*] him into the wilderness [or "desert"]." (1:10, 12)

One of my favorite phrases for connecting and introducing pericopes, i.e., more or less self-contained units of oral or written material which I had at my disposal, was the phrase "and he said to them." (2:27; 3:23; 4:2, 11, 21, 24; 6:4, 10; 7:9, 14; 8:21; 9:1, 31; 11:17) In most of the cases where I use this linking-introductory phrase my purpose is to: (a) take the material out of a context within the tradition in which I found it and place it in a context I am creating; (b) indicate private information or special instruction given (by Jesus) to the disciples. The same is true of other similar phrases which I use. For example: "and he is saying [or says] to them" points to "esoteric arrangements that the disciples are to make (11.2), ...a private disclosure of his [Jesus'] supernatural powers (4.35), and of his mission (1.18) and... private instruction (4.13; 6.31, 50; 7.18; 10.11; 14.34)."[48]

Another phrase (from one Greek verb, *proskalein*) which I found particularly appropriate as an editorial connection, the significance of which my early readers/hearers could surely catch, was "he called to (him or himself)" (7:14; 3:23; 3:13; 6:7; 8:1; 8:34; 10:42; 12:43). In all but the first two of these instances it is clear that I intended to portray Jesus as giving special instruction or interpretation to his disciples alone. In these cases he calls his disciples aside, or away from the crowds. This is one of my methods for providing a special setting for particular words and deeds of Jesus and thereby giving them the special meaning I wanted them to have for my readers/hearers.[49]

I use two other Greek phrases (the synonyms *kata monas* and *kat'idian*) which indicate a situation of privacy. They are usually translated "alone" and "privately." I use these idioms to introduce words and deeds of Jesus which are made known to his disciples only: e.g., 4:10, 34; 13:3 ("explanation in private of public teaching"); 7:33; 9:28 ("healings performed out of the sight of the crowd"); 6:31f. ("an unsuccessful attempt at withdrawal and rest which culminates in the feeding of the multitude by the lake"); 9:2 (which "introduces the story of the special vision of Jesus exalted with Moses and Elijah"), i.e. the "Transfiguration."[50]

All of these editorial interpretive connections ("and he said to them," "and he is saying to them," "he called to him" or "to himself," "alone," and "privately") implicitly suggest that: (a) even though the disciples did not, or could not, understand correctly the full meaning of Jesus until after the crucifixion and resurrection, nevertheless they were given special, private, "esoteric" instructions and illustrations of the meaning of his person, words, and actions; (b) all subsequent "disciples," while being called into and given a special community in relation to Jesus, *must also* understand him and relate to him (as well as to one another and to the world) only from this perspective, i.e., the perspective of faith informed by the crucifixion and the resurrection; (c) the minority community of "the disciples" in my age (or any age)—my (the) Christian community—precisely *as disciples* (cf. 3:13–15; 6:7–13; 8:34–9:1) will be given, *is given*, insight, understanding, awareness, and *experience of the truth* of the Gospel that simply is not available to the many others who do not follow Jesus, believe in the Gospel, and share in this community life of discipleship, defined by cross and empty tomb. Certain profound truths are known, certain eternal realities are experienced only as one actively follows the Lord.

Since I have already told you that all the warps and wefts of the tapestry of my Gospel are interwoven with one another, it will come as no surprise to you now if I mention that this implicit significance of these interpretive connections introducing private instruction is essentially the same as that of Jesus' prohibitions to those who would openly make known who he was before the "conclusion-continuation" of his story. I intentionally present Jesus, on numerous occasions, but not consistently, as *commanding* silence about his identity: e.g., the man with "the unclean spirit," 1:23; other "unclean spirits," 3:11; "demons," 1:34; a man whom Jesus cured of leprosy, 1:43; Jairus, his wife and daughter, plus the others "who were with them" after Jesus had raised the child from her "death" bed, 5:43; the people present when Jesus healed the man who was deaf and had an impediment in his speech, 7:36; a blind man whom Jesus healed at Bethsaida (?), 8:26; the disciples after Peter's confession of Jesus as "the Christ," 8:30; the disciples after the "transfiguration" experience, 9:9.

In this same drama-story, as I composed it, you will, however, also read how Jesus did powerful and wonderful acts of healing physical infirmities (2:1–12; 3:1–6; 5:24–34; 6:56; 7:24–30), casting out demons (5:1–20; 7:24–30), and feeding people (6:30–44; 8:1–10) without admonishing anyone not to tell about it. In fact, in one case you will read that after he had exorcised a "legion" of demons from one man Jesus even commanded him to " 'Go home to your friends, and tell them how much the Lord has done for you, and how he has had mercy on you.' And he went away and began to proclaim in the Decapolis how much Jesus had done for him; and all men marveled." (5:19–20) On many occasions Jesus makes no attempt to teach the inner circle of his disciples only and in secret. Rather he openly teaches the crowds and various classes of people (e.g., 6:1; 6:6; 11:17; 14:49). In some cases Jesus' identity is at least implied openly by others (e.g., 1:7; 1:11; 1:28[?]; 6:7–13) or by himself (e.g., 1:17; 2:10, 20, 28; 11:1–10; 13:6, 21; *14:62).

A generation ago many of your New Testament scholars were pondering perplexedly the blatant inconsistency which these references make obvious and trying to explain it. On the assumption that I had written an objective, although selective, "historical" account of the "main events" of the last year or

The Messianic Secret

years of Jesus' earthly life, they were hard pressed to solve the problem. Was the command to silence about his identity a definitive and general characteristic of "the historical Jesus"? If so, was it then merely that some of the early and continuing reports of Jesus' words and deeds simply failed to include this characteristic element? But if it was consistent and characteristic why would it not be reported in each and every instance of its expression? Was Jesus himself inconsistent? Was he selective to whom he disclosed his real identity? Perhaps to the disciples only, to whom he secretly reinterpreted the meaning of "Messiahship"? But what then do you do with cases like 2:10; 2:27; 3:20–28; 5:19–20; 11:1–10; and 14:62; clear implications or open declarations by Jesus of his special role and unique authority?

One German scholar, Professor Wilhelm Wrede, put the discussion on a new and right track when he suggested that *I* had written "the Messianic Secret" *into* my Gospel in order to explain to people in my day why more people in Jesus' day had not seen and accepted and believed in Jesus as the Messiah.[51] Professor Wrede was right about my writing "the command to silence" into the script of my "gospel of Jesus Christ, the Son of God," (1:1) but he was mistaken about the exact reason for and the meaning of my doing so. I wasn't trying to explain why something happened or didn't happen back then in Jesus' day so much as I was saying that you (anyone) can see, accept, and believe that Jesus is "the Christ" (Son of God, Son of man), and comprehend the real (God-intended) meaning of Jesus' Messiahship" aright, *only* from within the perspective offered, in faith, by the experiences of crucifixion and resurrection. *If* my evangelical and pastoral "passion play" is viewed as merely a historical account, then this theological-literary device *appears* to reflect historical and sequential facts: (1) inconsistency on the part of Jesus or within the tradition about him, and (2) the impossibility of understanding the meaning of this person and the history about him until it is experienced all the way through. I agree that (2) was true; but my main idea in writing Jesus' "command to silence" into my Gospel composition was to communicate something about the present more than the past. It was to say, again, that right now, as you read or hear and experience this Gospel remember that the only way it is good news, understandable and "experienceable" as such, is through suffering (death, crucifixion) unto new life (resurrection). *That* is "The Messianic Secret." And, as always, the big question is, "Can you hear it and accept it?"

As I mentioned previously in my discussion of the titles of Jesus, one of my favorite designations for him was "teacher." This is the specific title I used for him most often. I did not intend, however, to suggest that Jesus was your regular Rabbi employing the standard rabbinical pedagogical methods. He was much more than that. Although he could engage other teachers effectively in disputation (12:13–34), he did not rely solely on secondary source authorities as they did. He spoke with his *own* authority (1:21f.). As a teacher both he and his teaching were different in other ways. Not only his method of instruction but also the content of the teaching was distinctive. This is one of the important reasons he got into trouble with the scribes and Pharisees. Yes, he taught in parables, short metaphorical stories, which offered insight into the "extraordinary" through "ordinary" situations and events within common life (e.g., 4:1–9). But he also taught through "parabolic" or "pedagogical" dramatic *acts* (e.g., 1:21–22; 4:38; 5:35; 6:34; 9:17; 9:38; 11:21). If you wish to grasp this portrait of Jesus, with its multiple manifestations, as I present it in my Gospel, just read through the drama again pausing and pondering on the places where he functions as teacher, asking: What is he saying? How is he saying it? What is he doing? How is he doing it? These are the main passages to peruse: 1:21–28; 2:13–3:6; 3:7–31; 4:1–41; 5:1–43; *6:1–6; 6:30–44; 7:1–23; 8:11–21, 31–9:50; *10:1–45; 10:46–52; 11:12–33; 12:1–11; 12:13–44; 13:1–32; 14:12–25, *49. That's just about all of my Gospel again, isn't it? This is another illustration of how structural motifs and theological themes overlap and interlace one another in my drama. But I didn't intend to get off so far into the theme of "Jesus as Teacher." What I was about to do was simply to point out that references to Jesus as teacher and to his activity as teaching are prominent in the editorial framework of my Gospel (e.g., 1:21f.; 2:13; 4:1f.; 4:33; 6:1; 6:34; 8:31, 34; 9:31; *10:1, 17, 35; 11:17; 12:13, 18, 35, *38; 13:1).

I will mention just one more kind of editorial connection I employed with partiality and purpose in the composition of my little apocolyptic pamphlet. This is an appropriate designation for my document, for it signifies a kind of writing which attempts to disclose, or pull back the curtain on a supra-historical, cosmic drama that is taking place. "Apocalyptic" comes from the Greek word *apocalypsis* from which we get our words "apocalypse" and "revelation" (like The Apocalypse or Revelation to John). It originally signified the lifting of a veil. For me the meaning of *apocalyptic* can best be illustrated by the drawing back of the curtain on the stage of one of your modern theaters so the audience can see what is going on in the play, so that this side can get in on what is happening on that side. The supreme significance of the apocalyptic drama which my pamphlet is about is that (a) it is, *the* definitive, cosmic show, the play that discloses the real meaning of all previous, concurrent, and future earthly episodes; and (b) it is the drama to end all dramas, it is the final (eschatological) act. Paradoxically it is also the *beginning* of a whole new scene. Yet this drama has really been going on for generations within the history of God's people of the old covenant, the people of Israel, the Jews.

It was reenacted representatively, faithfully, through that one true Jew ("Son of David," 10:47, 48; 11:10) who fulfilled its true, inherent meaning. In order to do this it was necessary for him to recover that original meaning, reinterpret the tradition, and correct the contemporary. This he did by both words and deeds. And the result was a new covenant, a new people, a new history, a new story, a new drama, which is, significantly, already past, present, and future. I was not the first one to be influenced by such ideas when it came to developing a presentation about the meaning of human existence. Although my Gospel, strictly speaking, as a literary genre, was a first, unique, I was familiar with and heavily influenced, both in form and content, structure and meaning, symbol and sense by earlier Jewish apocalyptic writing, especially the Old Testament book of Daniel. That's the first place from which I get my title for Jesus as "Son of man." The book of Daniel (ca. 165 B.C.) is an apocalyptic pamphlet, too, which also, in a pre-dated disguised fashion, was claiming to be telling it like it *really* was, to be saying what was *really* happening and about to happen regardless of what the contemporary scene of historical events and human existence looked like. I drew ideas and symbols from other Jewish apocalypses also, but it was Daniel, mainly, that I was saying my apocalyptic pamphlet, or more precisely the eschatological drama it presents, fulfilled.[52]

But back to the main point here: one little Greek word which I used partially and purposively to heighten the dramatic atmosphere and the dramatic effect of my Gospel. That Greek word is a verb, *archomai,* and it means "to begin." It is used as a helping verb (often with the infinitive "to teach"). I chose it and employed it tellingly in the editorial or introductory framework of individual passages and in interpretive connections between passages (e.g., 1:45; 2:23; 4:1; 5:20; 6:2, 7, 34, 55; 8:11, 31, 32; 10:32; 11:15; 12:1; 13:5). I also used this word often *within* passages (5:17; 10:18, 41, 47; 14:19, 33, 65, 71; 15:8, 18). From my use of this word at these junctures, within these contexts, pointing as it does in most cases to an action of Jesus (verbal or physical), or the consequences of his action, I wanted to suggest to you not just a feeling or a mood, but also something like this: if *that* was the beginning of all these things then what is this? The *continuing.* If *that* was the beginning of the ending of the old age and the beginning of the beginning of the new age, then where are we *now*? In the continuing of this interim act, headed toward its ending and the beginning of the completely and never-ending new age.[53]

Now let me remind you of some summary statements which I include in my Gospel and suggest some possible, appropriate outlines for studying it.

Summaries

I can really be brief here. Most of the summaries serve a dual function, both to summarize and to connect to what has gone before and/or what is to follow (e.g., 1:14–15, 32–34, 39; 2:1–2, 13, 15; 4:1, 32–34; 6:56; 8:31; 10:1). Some, in fact, summarize, connect, and *introduce* what's coming next (e.g., 1:1–15; 4:1; 3:33–35; 8:31; 10:1). Most of my summaries can be grouped broadly under the following headings: "Jesus' Preaching Repentance, the Word, the Gospel" (1:14–15, 39; 2:1–2); "The Disciples Preaching the Same Message," (3:14; 6:12–13); "Jesus Teaching" (2:13; 3:23; 4:1, 33–34; 6:6*b*; 8:31, 21–26; 9:31; 10:1; 12:1; 13:1–5*a*); "Jesus Healing the Sick and Casting Out Demons" (1:32–34, 39; *3:7–12); "The Disciples of Jesus Doing the Same" (6:13, 54–56). The point I'm trying to make is that even through redactional or editorial devices I was trying to get my message across; I wasn't wasting any words. And by the way I was putting them together and *where* I was putting them I intended to signal meaning. Jesus was and *is* the proclaimer of the good news as well as the one who is proclaimed (e.g., 6:12). *He is* the Teacher now, through those who rightly teach in his name. This teaching may occur through writings, such as my Gospel, as well as through speaking directly to individuals and groups such as my community, e.g., 6:30. His teaching now, as then, is defined by the theme of suffering through death unto resurrection (life, 8:31f.). We are all his pupils. As the master goes, so go the students (disciples, 8:34–9:1). He is still, as he was, the healer and exorcist, through *all* those who in his name (9:38–39) bring health, wholeness, and freedom from possessive and destructive powers (3:13–15; 6:7–13).

Outlines

I said earlier that I would give you an outline which you can use in studying my Gospel, if you so desire, and I suggested that such an outline might be helpful. But now I've got a problem. As you probably have gathered from what I have told you thus far about the way I put some of the disconnected units of my raw material together to form my composite document, I had more than one meaningful arrangement in mind. Even in separate or distinct sections, such as chapter 13, the so-called "Synoptic Apocalypse," and chapters 11–16, the so-called "Passion Narrative" or " Passion Week," I freely but purposefully connected and wove together oral/written tradition which was available to me along with my own personal perceptions. (One urgent concern I had in my creative redaction of these two sections, specifically and especially, was to demonstrate how the story of Jesus and his followers, past, present, and future, was a fulfillment of Old Testament historical hope and prophetic insight–but with a difference). I doubt seriously if even I could precisely sort out one source from another in these passages, or others for that matter. It was a long time ago! I know for certain, however, that your scholars have labored long and hard in the effort to do just that. Part of the cause for the difficulty is the freedom which I felt and exercised in the use of my sources. My creativity was not inhibited by a rigid doctrine of verbal inspiration, or an awesome awareness that I was writing holy scripture. As I said in the beginning, I was *convinced* that Jesus though crucified, dead, and buried, had been resurrected and was alive and speaking and acting through us his faithful followers within our community and within our world (e.g., 3:13–15, 20–35; 4:10–34; 6:7–13, 30; 9:33–37, 38–41, 42–50; 10:20–25; 12:25; 13:9–13, 14–23; 16:1–8). As an expression of this conviction and its consequent freedom I composed my Gospel! But back to outlines.

Of course the intention of the scholars has been to discern my outline and to disclose it, not to impose on my document an outline that I didn't have in mind. Often however, the latter has happened. Again, part of the problem is that I was weaving my tapestry with more than one single design pattern. In a real sense, therefore, you could trace any of my several themes through my Gospel and each would be an appropriate outline, one that emerges, or surfaces naturally from the document because it was written into it.

There *are* some large overarching frameworks, however, which I used, which are fairly obvious, and which numerous of your scholars have discovered. For example, there is a "profesion of faith" outline with my announcement of "the gospel of Jesus Christ, the Son of God," *at the beginning* (1:1); Peter's confession of Jesus as "the Christ" *in the middle* (8:29); and the confession of the centurian that "truly this man was a [or the] son of God" (15:39) near the end. If you trace the use of the christological title "Son of God" (or "Son") exclusively, another beginning, middle, ending pattern appears: 1:1, 10–11; 9:2–8; 15:39 (see also 3:11; 5:7; 14:61). Obviously Peter's confession in the center of the Gospel is a focal point. Some scholars have suggested that I portray Jesus as presenting his message through his words and deeds *publicly* to everyone from 1:14 through 8:26 (after the introduction of 1:1–13) and from that point on (8:27), perhaps because of disappointment with his lack of success and abundance of conflict (opposition), *privately* to his inner circle of disciples only, until his arrest and their forsaking of him (14:50). This two-fold division, including the prologue of 1:1–13, would be concluded with the important epilogue of 14:53–16:8 ("trials," crucifixion, and resurrection).

Geographical outlines have been popular among students of my Gospel. And I must admit that they are legitimate if it is recognized that they are more literary-theological than they are historico-geographical. If you will read carefully through my document you will notice that, along with all the definite, accurate, and sequential place designations[54] there are also some rather vague, general, or indefinite location references (e.g., 1:35; 2:13, 15, 23; 3:1, 7, 13, 19*b*; 6:1, 30, 47; 7:14; 10:17; 11:19), and even some geographical mistakes (6:45–53; 7:31) and confusions (4:35 and 5:1; 5:20–21).[55] These indefinite location references, geographical mistakes and confusions indicate clearly that (1) some of my sources were geographically uncertain and confused, or (2) I was not completely familiar with Palestinian geography, or (3) some of my sources were not primarily concerned with historico-geographical accuracy, or (4) I was not primarily concerned with historico-geographical accuracy, or (5) any combination of some of the above, or (6) *all* of the above. Would you believe number 6?

However, a rough and broad outline of movement consisting of place references did serve me in my structural-conceptual or literary-theological purpose. I was doing theology (Christology) through literary use of geographical references. Jesus delivers his message indiscriminately to the world, universally (1:14—8:26), then privately to a select few, his disciples (8:27—9:50), then in Judea (10:1), the realm of Jewish orthodoxy, and finally, of necessity, in Jerusalem, the center of religious and civil authority ("on the way to Jerusalem," as are all his disciples, 10:17, 32, 46; 11:1, and in Jerusalem, 11:11—16:8, with side trips to Bethany, 11:11-12; 14:3). As I portray the story, the main character must move from the perimeter to the center of the circle of conflict in order to join the issue in the decisive sphere, to faithfully engage the opposition in the citadel of its power, in the necessary manner and mode of his mission (vulnerable but strong, exposed but victorious, suffering unto death but resurrected unto life).

Yes, this does correspond roughly and generally to the way it happened historically and geographically. But the theological meaning was of more importance to me! If you do not overlook the "thematic shifts" within it, and you interpret it more theologically than historically, the outline by Professor Vincent Taylor can be quite helpful in organizing one approach to my Gospel.[56]

    1:1–13   Introduction
    1:14–3:6   Galilean Ministry
    3:7–6:13   Height of Galilean Ministry

6:14–8:26	Ministry Beyond Galilee
8:27–10:52	Caesarea Philippi. Journey to Jerusalem
11:1–13:37	Ministry in Jerusalem
14:1–16:8	Passion and Resurrection

Another outline suggested recently which, I feel, comes more out of my document than out of the presuppositions of the scholar, is that of Professor Norman Perrin:[57]

1:1–13	Introduction
1:14–15	Transitional Markan Summary
1:16–3:6	Authority of Jesus in Word and Deed
3:7–12	Transitional Markan Summary
3:13–6:6a	Jesus as Son of God and Rejected by His People
6:6b	Transitional Markan Summary
6:7–8:21	Jesus as Son of God: Misunderstood by His Disciples
8:22–26	Transitional Gaining of Sight Story
8:27–10:45	Christology and Discipleship in Light of the Passion
11:1–12:44	Days in Jerusalem Prior to the Passion
13:1–5a	Introduction to the Apocalyptic Discourse
13:5b–37	Apocalyptic Discourse
14:1–12	Introduction to the Passion Narrative
14:13–16:8	Passion Narrative

If these outlines help you to recognize my theological motifs, then I recommend them to you. However, it would probably be better to look for my different (but related) theme-designs as I weave them through my Gospel tapestry. It would also help to explore the meaning of individual passages within their larger literary contexts, for they are varied expressions of belief from my first-century Christian community.

Well, I can see by the empty hour glass on the lectern here that our time has more than run out. Ahem! I can also see, Professor, that there is no one left here in the hall but you and me. So I'd better stop talking and leave my Gospel in your and your students' hands. Treat it carefully and responsibly, please. And what I said before I now say to you, "and what I say to you I say to all: *gregorèite! Watch!" (13:37) Shalom. Eirène.* Peace (5:34).

PART III:

St. Mark

Heard

Now that Mark has spoken and explained to us, in part, how he put his book together in order to communicate several of his major themes and minor motifs, let us approach his Gospel in a more familiar fashion. Let us explore in some detail one ovcrarching theological message. This message is clarified by our literary and thematic analysis and is understood further by a brief excursion into the general background—historical, cultural, and religious—of this document. After this we will engage in interpretive reflections on fourteen representative sections.

Christ and Conflict:
An Essay on a Theme

The Gospel According to Mark might be appropriately subtitled "Christ and Conflict." For Mark, its composer, his first century community, and for generations of Christians ever since, it is the glad and confident proclamation that in the universal struggle between God (salvation, freedom, and life) and Satan (sin, bondage, and death), God, through his Son, Jesus of Nazareth, is the Victor. Originally declared in his words and demonstrated in his deeds, it is the astonishing announcement of the Man from Galilee to the Jews of Palestine in their day that, all evidence to the contrary not withstanding (Roman legions, captivating demons, inhibiting regulations), *God* is the Ruler of this world. Those who turn to him, trusting this message (1:15) and following him, are both secure *in him* and responsible *to him,* now, in the midst of a precarious earthly existence (4:35–41; 6:45–50; 8:34–38; 13) as well as in the age to come (10:28–31). For those who first hear him preaching "the kingdom" (1:15) and teaching "with authority" (1:22; 10:1); who first watch him liberating the possessed (1:25), healing the diseased (1:34), and wresting humanity from the death-grip of the evil one, the destroyer (3:19–27); who follow him as his way of direct relation and open association with anyone leads him into a clash with the preservers of the socio-religious *status quo* (2:13–3:6); who see him crucified by those whose *self*-security (power, position, and prestige) is threatened by his claiming presence and all-embracing love (14:53–15:32); who become convinced that he is yet alive and going before them into Galilee (16:1–8), *before them into their world and their history, there to meet them and involve them in his continuing work*—in short, for those early witnesses and members of the emerging church, it is the amazing affirmation of long-delayed hope fulfilled, the end of the old and the beginning of the new. It is celebration today and hope looking forward to tomorrow.

A generation later, when the Gospel of Mark was written, it is the deeply encouraging word to the Christians of the first-century Roman world that although they are caught in conflict within the church and without, *Christus Victor* is also the great Reconciler. Although they are exiled, imprisoned, and exterminated they are, nevertheless, safe, free, and alive as they remain faithful to him, his word, and his way (8:31–38; 10:34–45; 13).

For Christians today, in an age of astronauts and anxiety, limitless space and cramped global quarters, affluence and poverty, overweight and starvation, stability and revolution, proposals for peace and death on the battlefield, confident technology and dreary assembly-line existence, limitless human potential and dwindling natural resources, salvation and lostness—in the current era of conflict, for those who believe it, Mark has a message of penetrating meaning. Again, all evidence to the contrary notwithstanding, *God rules.* This is his world. In and through Christ, his Son, he is yet alive, victorious, authoritative, and active in the world—saving, liberating, forgiving, reconciling, healing, nourishing, and giving life (10:45). He is still encouraging, supporting, and strengthening those involved in the struggle; he is still calling women and men to believe this tremendous declaration, to follow him, *and to participate with him in his saving action* (6:7–13) *here and now.*

This is a brief summary of the essential elements of one major message which runs through the Gospel of Mark, as it is apprehended and communicated in its universal dimension and its Palestinian, Roman, and contemporary contexts. In the story of Jesus as Mark interprets it, the development of this theme can be clearly seen. This conflict in which Christ is engaged and from which he emerges victorious *begins* with his temptation (1:12f.); it *heightens* as he forcefully casts out the demons (1:21–28, etc.); it *continues to mount* as his sabbath healings (e.g., 3:1–6) and disputations about the validity of legal religious tradition bring upon him the hostility of the scribes and the Pharisees (e.g., 2:18–28; 7:1–23) who set about to destroy him; it *reaches a peak* in his cleansing of the Temple (11:15–19); it is *climaxed* in his dark night of struggle in Gethsemane (14:32–50); it is *concluded* in his trial and crucifixion (14:53–15:39); and it is *overcome* in his resurrection (16:1–8), by which it is shown that he is, *indeed,* the Victor.

In order that we may more clearly and more fully understand how this message may be translated into the categories of our current life, let us consider it in further detail under the following four headings: Conflict in the Cosmos, Conflict in Palestine, Conflict in the Roman World, and Conflict in Contemporary Culture.

Conflict in the Cosmos

A dualistic understanding of the universe, or cosmos, was widely held in the ancient world during the Hellenistic Era, the period of approximately 200

B.C. to 100 A.D. It is called "Hellenistic" because practically all of its cultural characteristics, such as language, literature, philosophy, religion, and art, were leftovers from the Greeks, the Hellenes, of an earlier day. These contributions of civilization had been spread over Asia Minor, the Middle East, and as far into the Orient as Northern India during the years 333 B.C. to 323 B.C. by the brilliant conqueror from Macedonia, Alexander the Great, lover of all things Greek, whose tutor was Aristotle. By the first century A.D. and the time of the Roman Empire these residual aspects of Hellenism were the common property of most people of Western Europe, Asia Minor, the Middle East, and North Africa, having been adopted by the Romans and carried by soldiers and merchants to the farthest reaches of their world.

At the time of Jesus, and later when Mark wrote his Gospel, this popular dualism was a mixture of traits from Greek philosophy and Eastern religion. Indeed, its conceptual roots go back into the primitive-mythic soil of ancient Egypt, Babylon, and Mesopotamia. With essentially the same basic elements, but in a variety of forms, it dominated the outlook of Greeks, Jews, Romans, and Easterners alike. Simply put, it was the belief in two cosmic realms of power and influence: Heaven above, which is the abode of Deity, the sphere of light, goodness, and life, from whence the angels (or other emissaries of God) go forth among people upon earth to do the divine command; and Hell (or Hades) below, the abode of Satan, the sphere of darkness, evil, and death, from whence the demons go forth among humans to do their diabolical business. These two realms are at odds; they are in conflict. Each would possess the world and humankind (individual persons).

There was some difference of opinion as to just how long this situation had existed. Some (mostly Persians and Greeks) thought that the universe had consisted of these two opposed forces since the beginning of time. This point of view we might call absolute dualism. Others (particularly the Jews, but also some Greeks) understood that at the outset the universe was the creation of God and therefore essentially (or as God had made it and intended it to be) *good* (Gen. 1:31). But, as human existence in every historical present witnessed—as pain, and sin, and ignorance, and evil, and suffering, and death all evidenced—something had happened. Creation had "fallen." From earliest times this tragedy was explained (symbolized) most commonly by reference to the primordial anti-God beast, or personal Tempter (Gen. 3) who had revolted against the Divine, or duped human beings into insurrection, or both. By the first century A.D., in both Eastern religions and Western philosophies this fall had become associated primarily with insubordinate beings or rebellious angels. It was the belief of many that the inhabited world was temporarily under the control of this Evil One, that the present age was under the domination of the Devil and his cohorts. This mythic description was symbolic of a state of being. But it was also held that because the whole universe and all its inhabitants were first and finally God's, this current state of affairs could not last indefinitely. The conflict was now joined, but God must ultimately be the winner. He would set things right again. How and when he was to do this (or had done it, or was doing it) were questions which distinguished the faiths of first century people. But the primary point of agreement among those who fit into this second category of dualism is the conviction that things had not always been thus, that the present cosmic contention was a perversion of the original pattern of divinely ordained existence, that the gap could be bridged or the conflict overcome. We may call this temporary dualism.

In either case, however, human beings find themselves on the horizontal plane, on the earth, between the two opposing forces, above and below. And to a greater or lesser degree humankind is at the mercy of the powers of evil or Satan, and his enslaving demonic spirits. What are human beings to do in this situation? They can, of course, hopelessly acquiesce in their plight, impotently adjust to their predicament. Or they can try to get out of it, to escape. If people choose to pursue this latter alternative they may join one of the religious or philosophical movements of the day which offer to help people bridge the gap between the two realms. For example, people may enlist in the community of a mystery religion. Here they will engage in ritual washings and a baptism of purification; they will undergo a secret initiation; they will identify with a mythical redeemer deity; and by these means they will hope to attain the salvation of their souls, the assurance of the immortality of their inner beings, and their return to their celestial home upon the death of their bodies. In this present life they will be satisfied with serenity in the midst of conflict. Or people may seek release as members of a gnostic sect. Here they will gain true *gnosis,* they will acquire right *knowledge.* Through the dramatic myth of the heavenly "Man" who comes from above to enlighten them, they will learn that both the source and the nature of their real spiritual "selves" are divine, that the world of material decay and all that goes with it is the work of sub-deities lesser than God and is, therefore, not quite real. It is a somewhat illusory trap in which they are caught. But, they are promised, by heeding this true knowledge and by engaging in the proper worship and the appropriate religious exercises, they may gain their freedom, rise above this physical existence, return to the realm of the Divine, and realize again their true selves.

Or, first-century people, especially if they are Jewish, may wait expectantly for *God* to act. Painfully aware that humans are *not* able to save themselves, unconvinced that nonhistorical deities are potent enough to do what is needed, confirming the reality, original goodness, and indivisibility of the created world of spirit and matter, soul and flesh, and knowing from experience that more than knowledge is necessary, their only hope is that God will conclude the conflict, defeat the adversary, redeem the world, and save humankind. This, the Gospel of Mark claims is precisely what has happened in Christ. In and through him, his life, death, and resurrection, the Enemy, which, in a variety of guises, would enslave humanity and cripple people and do them to death has been dealt the decisive blow. The battle has been won. This is the glad good news. And it may be just as meaningful for the Greek or Roman as it is for the Jew, for both are victims caught in the cosmic conflict.

In his authoritative words and authoritative actions, Jesus demonstrated that he was God's representative. He announced the kingdom of God and he personified it. Therefore, those who followed him preached that in and through him it had been surely established. Granted, it still waits to be consummated (8:38–9:1; 13). The back of the Beast has been broken, but he refuses to quit thrashing around and admit that he is vanquished. His forces, obstinately and destructively, refuse to lay down their arms. And in this new meantime, therefore, the conflict continues. But the outcome is certain and soon (9:1; 13:25, 30); and the quality of this present is determined by God's imminent future. Consequently, those who believe, who trust Jesus Christ, have nothing now to fear (4:35–41). Those who follow him, who identify with him, who let their *lives* be defined by his *death,* have nothing to lose and everything to gain (8:34f.). Those who love as he loved (e.g., 6:34; 10:21; 12:28–34) are already safe, free, and truly alive, regardless of what happens to them (13:9–13). Not even death itself can threaten them (13:12f.). This is gospel.

For the most part this Gospel has been proclaimed (even in the explanation above) in ancient cosmic categories, in thought-forms of the first century A.D. We no longer, however, live in a three-storied world: heaven above, hell below, and earth in the middle. On the contrary, some scientists say, ours is "an ever expanding universe." Two spatial realms of existence (up and down) no longer comprise the conceptual frame of reference in which we ordinarily operate. At least six days a week (and most of the seventh) most people today are really concerned only with the here and the now. Not many of us actually believe in the existence of demons today (recent popular novels and movies to the contrary notwithstanding!). And the concept of "a personal Devil" is difficult for most modern people to hold in a literal fashion.

Does this mean that the message which is communicated through these ancient cosmic ("mythic") categories and first-century thought-forms is itself no longer meaningful or comprehensible? If science since the days of Copernicus and Galileo has been correct does this disprove the Word of God? Many New Testament scholars and students would reply: Only if we equate this eternal Word with the historically conditioned and temporary cosmology and language symbols of the biblical era. But this we need not do. Indeed, this is a false equation. The Gospel *has* its stumbling block which cannot and should not be removed, but one only: the Cross (1 Cor. 1:23; Gal. 5:11). A cosmology which modern people can no longer honestly use need not, however, stand in our way or trip up our understanding. We in fact can, and surely must, bring across the unchanging truth which is couched in and conveyed through the primitive, mythic worldview, by translating this cosmic dualism into concepts and words which are meaningful for us today. This will be attempted to a greater extent in the sections below. At this point it may simply be suggested that a brief and tentative interpretation might run like this: God, in and through Jesus Christ, has openly declared and demonstrated that this is *his* world, that life in him (life in a total sense) has the final word over death, that *he* is in control of human history and *presently* at work in the world giving this life, through Christ, in a variety of ways, that those who would respond to Christ's call "follow me" (1:16–20) are to identify and locate this action of God and participate in it wherever it is and in whatever form it is currently expressed, that by trusting God in Christ and obeying him ("Thou shalt love") any person may share in this life now and forever (cf. 12:28–34; 8:31–37; 10:17–22).

Questions and Suggestions

Does the last sentence above have real meaning for you? Do you think it even begins to translate accurately the significance of Jesus' proclamation of the kingdom of God and Mark's portrayal of the victory of God in Christ within the cosmic conflict? Do you actually believe (operate on this basis seven days a week) in a spatial heaven which is up and a physical hell which is down? Do you believe in the existence and activity of a personal, spiritual devil? When ordering your normal life, do you ever consider the possibility of the existence and activity of angels or demons? Is it *necessary* to use these first-century concepts and categories in order to rightly and truthfully communicate the meaning of Jesus' announcement of the kingdom of God and Mark's proclamation of Christ's cosmic victory?

It might be helpful to attempt right now to write out a brief statement which you think would communicate the salvation significance of the cosmic victory of Christ without using spatial terms and categories of thought which are appropriate to a three-layered universe but not to the modern scientific worldview. As you study the individual passages from Mark for the separate interpretive reflections, particularly those where the message is cast in terms of heaven, hell, angels, and demons, ask yourself how you might accurately express the true meaning of the biblical text, for yourself and other people today, using other words and phrases.

Conflict in Palestine

Not only does the Gospel of Mark confront the reader with a conflict in the cosmos in which Christ is the victor, but it also reflects a conflict between Jesus and Jewish authorities in the land of Palestine. As Mark presents it, this conflict begins with the clash between Jesus and the scribes over his "authority to forgive sins." (2:1–12) It increases in the collision between Jesus and the scribes of the Pharisees caused by his open association with the religiously and socially unacceptable (2:13–17). It intensifies in his continued controversy with the Pharisees over the nature and observance of the law (e.g., 2:23–3:6). It ends with Jesus' arrest, trial, and crucifixion (14:43–15:39).

Basically this is a conflict between the old order and the new (2:18–22), and, as Mark records it, it is focused in three revolutionary attitudes of Jesus which issue into action offensive to the guardians of the establishment: Jesus' attitude of *authority;* his attitude of open *receptivity;* his attitude of *freedom* from legal tradition. Let us look briefly at each of these contentions seeking to understand its original and permanent significance.

In the familiar story of The Roof Paralytic (2:1–12), as he heals the man, Jesus pronounces that his sins are forgiven (2:5). This event takes place at Capernaum, where Jesus was making his temporary residence (2:1), and it is preceded by his preaching of the Word. (2:2) What was this *word,* which is here not further defined? It must have been the fullness of that original announcement, "The kingdom of God is at hand; repent, and believe in the gospel." (1:15) Now this word is *acted out* in the healing of a crippled body, and spoken in another way: "My son, your sins are forgiven." (2:5) It was commonly thought among the Jews at this time that deformity and disease were the results of sin (cf. John 9:1–2). Operating within this conceptual context, Jesus pronounces the forgiveness of the paralytic's sins as equivalent to an active word of healing (2:10). By this spoken and embodied word Jesus could have simply been saying that now, within this New Age, *within the reign of God, human existence for the person of faith is characterized by forgiveness and wholeness of life.* It is highly significant that, as Mark presents the episode, "the word," "faith," "forgiveness," and "healing" are closely associated. Nor should we so center our attention upon the internal experience of forgiveness that we overlook the external fact that the paralyzed man was enabled to get up *physically,* take up his pallet, and walk away. This characterization of life in the age of God's reign would be meaning enough. But Mark apparently intends to communicate more.

Some of the scribes questioned "in their hearts, 'Why does this man speak thus? It is blasphemy! Who can forgive sins but God alone?' " (2:6) Then Jesus, "perceiving in his spirit that they thus questioned within themselves, said to them, 'Why do you question thus in your hearts? Which is easier, to say to the paralytic, "Your sins are forgiven," or to say, "Rise, take up your pallet and walk?" But that you may know that the Son of man has authority on earth to forgive sins'—he said to the paralytic—'I say to you, rise, take up your pallet and go home.' " (Mark 2:8–11) The dominant meaning of this passage now becomes clear. Not only is Jesus saying verbally and demonstrating actively that existence for the person of faith under God's reign is characterized by forgiveness of sin and wholeness of life, but he is also asserting the *authority* necessary to make this claim. And the only authority by which such a claim can be made is God. Such an assertion would naturally not go unquestioned by the scribes, the preservers and interpreters of God's traditional word, the sacred Torah, the holy Law. We can understand their reaction. And yet, according to Mark, *Jesus both defines the nature of existence under God and assumes authority in the present for participation in this new order.* It is as one is related to Jesus in faith that one is in fact a citizen of the kingdom of God and a recipient of the benefits available therein. Therefore, if a person is a follower of this Authoritative One, who, indeed, functions as the representative of God himself, he or she can but rejoice, even as wedding guests must feast, rather than fast, in the presence of the bridegroom (2:18-20).

This authority of Jesus, which offends the keepers of the old order, and which is underscored in several places in Mark (e.g., 1:22; 6:7; 7:6-8; 11:27-12:40), may have as much significance for us today as it did for those who first witnessed it. The application of its contemporary meaning is not simple. The specific expression–in word or in deed–may vary with different situations offering particular opportunities and making peculiar demands. But finally, in any and every case, for those who believe it, it will mean that *when the two are in irreconcilable conflict* " 'We must obey God rather than men.' " (Acts 5:29)

In 2:13-17 the author of this Gospel uses a story about Jesus which illustrates his attitude of *open receptivity*. Jesus calls Levi, a despised tax collector, to become a follower, and with his disciples he eats with "tax collectors and sinners," either as a guest in Levi's home, or as the host in his own house. (The text in 2:15 is not quite clear as to whose house is meant. It can be read either way. If Jesus is the host the incident is all the more remarkable.)

Capernaum was a border town in northeastern Galilee. It was on the main trade route which ran from Damascus, through Philip's territory of Gaulonitis, by way of Galilee, over a pass in the Mt. Carmel range, along the Plain of Sharon, through Gaza and on to Egypt. It was here in Capernaum that Levi was sitting in the customs office collecting the import and export charges. He was not directly in the service of the Romans. Therefore, he was not one of those Jews who had bought the franchise for tax gathering from the foreign ruler for a price, and he did not make his profit by squeezing from the taxpayers every cent he could get in order to raise his total receipts as high as possible above that sum required by the government official who owned him. Levi was probably in the employ of Herod Antipas, tetrarch of Galilee. It was his job to take up the toll levied on goods going out of and coming into this territory. If he could make the merchants pay more than the legal rate he could pocket the extra money. Since most of the common folk were never quite sure of the current tariff, it was not difficult to overcharge. In any case, Levi was an agent of the rich and oppressive traitor and a member of a well-hated class. As a tax collector, he was totally unacceptable, both religiously and socially, to the right kind of people. Jesus invited Levi to become a close friend. *They ate together!*

The sinners were those who failed to observe the Law. Some, undoubtedly, did not even keep all the basic moral injunctions of the Ten Commandments. Others, however, simply did not (or could not) abide by all the regulations of the scribes, such as abstinence from certain kinds of foods, ceremonial handwashing (7:1–23), or complete observance of the sabbath. These were the secular men of the day, the nonreligious types, the ordinary laborers, the poverty stricken outcasts, and the hardnosed businessmen. They did not recite the required formulas or practice the prescribed pieties. They were the unorthodox. They were called "the people of the land." (Cf. John 7:49.)

The Pharisees were the recognized and accepted religious leaders. Spiritual descendents of an earlier group called the Hasidim (the Separatists), the Pharisees in Jesus' day were those men who took their religion seriously. They kept the fundamental regulations of the law without exception. But beyond this they were concerned that the essence of God's will be done in every area of life. Therefore they sought to interpret and apply the inner meaning of the law to every situation a person might possibly face in the daily routine. In their effort to cover the whole of existence with perfect obedience they developed a long list of detailed rules. This body of minute legal injunctions came to be called "the tradition of the elders." (Cf. Mark 7:1–23.) It is doubtful that even they could keep all these requirements perfectly. But they *tried.* They held up the ideal. And everybody acknowledged that they were indeed the pious ones, the righteous, the orthodox.

The Pharisees looked down upon the tax collectors and the sinners and would have nothing to do with them. The Pharisees were, in fact, forbidden to associate with these people at all. They were "not [to] talk with them nor go on a journey with them"; as far as possible they were "not even [to] do business with them; to marry a daughter to one of them was as bad as giving her over to a wild beast"; above all they "must not accept hospitality or give hospitality to such a person."[1]

Needless to say, the tax collectors and sinners did not just naturally gravitate to the Pharisees! In fact, they must have felt quite ill at ease around them. In the collegiate parlance of several years back one would have said that the Pharisees gave the people of the land the freeze out. In the current idiom we might say that they put them down.

And, in turn, the tax collectors and sinners did not like the Pharisees. Apparently, however, they did like Jesus (2:15); and he must have liked them, for he associated with them a lot (cf. Luke 7:33f.). He called them to be his disciples and he openly received them. He did not condemn them, or reject them, or put them down. On the contrary, he *ate* with them. This is highly significant. For "to eat together meant that they would be bound by the mutual covenant of brotherhood, with all its obligations."[2] This is not to suggest, however, that Jesus condoned the attitudes and actions of these irreligious and lawless ones. He did not. But he showed deep concern for them, *exposed himself in vulnerable love to them,* and called them to repentance and entrance into life under God.

Given their separatist mind-set and their exclusive outlook it is not surprising that the scribes of the Pharisees asked the disciples of Jesus, " 'Why does he eat with tax collectors and sinners?' And when Jesus heard it, he said to them, 'Those who are well have no need of a physician, but those who are sick; I came not to call the righteous, but sinners.' " (2:16f.)

The contemporary relevance of this open receptivity of Jesus must by now be obvious. Regardless of what "the tradition" may say, followers of Jesus can be no less open and receptive and no more exclusive than he was. He welcomed all people. He appealed especially to the needy, to the religious and social outcasts. So must his disciples today. " 'A servant is not greater than his master.' " (John 13:16) Least of all can those who claim his name allow their religion, or use it, to erect barriers (religious, social, political) between God and people, or between their people and other people.

This discussion of Jesus' open receptivity which conflicted with the separatist exclusivism of the scribes of the Pharisees leads directly into a consideration of the continued controversy between Jesus and the Pharisees over the nature and observance of the Law. This dimension of the conflict in Palestine discloses Jesus' attitude of *freedom from death-dealing legalism to life-giving love.*

Much of what has already been said is applicable here. The Pharisees need not again be identified. Their concern for goodness, rightness, or righteousness, by obedience to the original and fundamental moral principles, has been stressed. The sincerity of their motive has been noted. Their attempt to make relevant the basic commands to every area of life by formulating rules to cover every situation has been observed. It must also now be underscored, however, that religion for the Pharisees had become essentially a matter of *externals.* Not only had they added to the Old Testament law, they had also perverted its original intention and use. During the early days of Israel the law of the covenant had been understood, accepted, and obeyed by the people as the definitive expression of their grateful *response* to God for the deliverance he had accomplished for them in the Exodus (Exod. 20:1–17). It was also that *commitment* which bound them and kept them vitally related to him who had brought them out of non-being into being and preserved them in their existence as a people (Exod. 19:3–6). As such, it was a kind of lifeline for them. It connected them with their source of breath, God himself. The numerous commandments which were developed during the generations succeeding the time of Moses all had as their central purpose to express grateful and responsive allegiance to the Lord and thereby to keep and give *life*. For only as the Hebrews lived in faithfulness to God did they live at all. To obey the Law was, therefore, the joy of a devout Hebrew's heart. Although from a somewhat later period, Psalm 119 expresses this feeling well: "Oh, how I love thy law! It is my meditation all the day." (Ps. 119:97)

The law was not originally given or received as a burden. But with their complex and complicated expansion of its basic commands, far beyond even that development which had occurred to a large extent during the Old Testament period (e.g., Exod. 21–22; Lev. 11–15; Deut. 14:1–15:23), the Pharisees had fashioned the law into a heavy yoke that could not be borne (cf. Matt. 11:29f.). Rather than a way unto life, it had become for most people an instrument of death.

Furthermore, the Pharisees made no practical distinction between their tradition and the commandments of the Old Testaments. To them they were all of equal authority. In the eyes of the orthodox it was just about as bad to pluck ears of corn (2:23–27) or heal a crippled body (both defined as forms of work) on the sabbath (3:1–6) as it was to murder someone. Jesus' reaction to this legalism of the Pharisees appears to be two-fold. First, he rejects the equation of the Old Testament law with the multiple and minute regulations of the Pharisees. This denial he makes both implicitly (by openly breaking these rules, e.g., in picking corn and healing on the sabbath) and explicitly ("'You leave the commandment of God, and hold fast the tradition of men.'" 7:8). Second, he goes back behind this fence to the word of God itself and recovers its original intent: to give and preserve life (2:27; 3:4).

The results of this attitude and action of Jesus are also two-fold. One: People are now responsible immediately to God. No longer, in order to be religious, are they bound to obey a check list of petty human precepts. They are free from conformity to externally imposed and traditional expectations. No longer need they engage in the anxiety-producing, paralyzing, and futile attempt at self-realization, self-security, and self-salvation through essentially other-directed decision and behavior. The questions, "Who am I" and "Am I acceptable (to God)" are not answered by who "they" say I should be and what "they" say I should do. Two: Real obedience to the law, in its horizontal expression within society, means simply meeting human needs, preserving and promoting wholeness of life. *Whatever* truly accomplishes this *is* lawful. "'The sabbath was made for man, not man for the sabbath.'" (2:27) The purpose of the original commandment to refrain from work on the seventh day was rest, refreshment, and restoration of energy for every laboring person and beast (Deut. 5:14). "And he said to them, 'Is it lawful on the sabbath to do good or to do harm, to save life or to kill?' But they were silent. And he looked around at them with anger, grieved at their hardness of heart, and said to the man, 'Stretch out your hand.' He stretched it out, and his hand was restored. The Pharisees went out, and immediately held counsel with the Herodians against him, how to destroy him." (3:4–6)

Finally, the *totality* of the law and the *sum* of practical religion (cf. Matt. 22:34–40) is a two-directional *love:* commitment of the whole self to God above all else, and active goodwill for the welfare of one's fellow persons, to the same degree and with the same intensity as one is presently concerned for one's self (Mark 12:29–31; cf. Luke 10:25–28). It is possible that these two commandments (Deut. 6:4–5 and Lev. 19:18) had already been linked together by Jewish teachers prior to Jesus' answer to the scribe's question (cf. Luke 10:25–28; Mark 12:28–33). If this was the case, then Jesus was calling the Jews to *do* what they *already knew.* But Jesus was saying more. There was a uniqueness about his characterization of this combination. " 'There is no other commandment greater than these.' " (12:31b) In other words, *all* other laws are subordinate to this two-fold love. And what is love if it is not preserving, promoting, and giving *life* in the fullest sense and in every possible way?

Some Questions for Further Reflection and Discussion

In what *areas* (e.g., religious, economic, political, social) and in what *ways* are individual Christians and the Christian church today acknowledging the authority of Jesus? In what areas and in what ways are they denying his authority and accepting the authority of others (the tradition of men)? Is it valid to divide life into separate areas, or should we think of it and attempt to live it as a unified whole under the authority of God? When the authority of God in Christ conflicts with the established authority of the human community (local, state, or national) what should Christians do? Can you give an example of a situation of this kind which has occurred or might occur within the church itself? How should the issue be decided? Are you aware of any social movements, political groups, or other secular organizations which claim religious (particularly Christian) sanction? Are they, in fact, under the authority of Christ or opposed to it as it is expressed in open receptivity and freedom to love? What should be the Christian's attitude toward such groups? Does the religion which we profess and practice express a grateful response to God and a preservation and promotion of life? Do we place requirements upon ourselves and others which are beyond the commandment of God and which therefore make it more difficult for us and others to obey the two-fold law of free and responsible love? Where would we have stood, what would have been our reaction to Jesus, if we had witnessed him exercising his authority, associating with and openly receiving "tax collectors and sinners," and disregarding the tradition of the religious establishment in order to truly fulfill the law?

Conflict in Rome

We now come to the third sphere in which this major theme of conflict reflected in Mark occurs. Broadly speaking, it is the Roman Empire of the first century A.D. More particularly it may have been the capital city itself. (It is highly probable that Mark's Gospel was received and used in Rome shortly after its publication.) Actually this single sphere is composed of three oppositions: congregation and synagogue, Gentile Christian and Jewish Christian, church and state. Contemporarily these manifestations of this sphere of conflict exist wherever and whenever similar conditions prevail. But in order to comprehend these controversies, in their original and current forms, it is necessary first to deal with two related matters: the authorship and the historical setting of the Gospel of Mark.

Authorship of Mark

Like most other questions of modern biblical scholarship, this one has been carefully studied and seriously debated for nearly a hundred years. At the present time there is no common consensus as to who the author of this Gospel was. But, generally, there are two alternatives: either he was John Mark, the sometime companion of Paul and perhaps also the colleague of Peter (1 Peter 5:13), or he was an unknown Jewish Christian living and writing outside of Palestine (perhaps in Syria). In either case our understanding of the *meaning* of this Gospel is not seriously affected.

Upon a close reading of this book it becomes evident that the author is addressing fellow Christians who are experiencing persecution without and controversy within the church. With this thought in mind read, for example, the following passages: 9:38–50; 12:13–17; 2:1–3:6; 7:1–23; 10:35–45; 8:34–9:1; 13. This kind of conflict setting would fit well with the situation in Rome about 65–75 A.D., which will be discussed briefly below.

There is an old and tenacious tradition within the church which associates John Mark closely with the Christian community in Rome (cf. Col. 4:10; 1 Pet. 5:13) and which claims that he is the author of this document. The question is still quite open, but supposing John Mark were the man finally responsible for this proclamation, what could we know about him? Assuming that *all* the references in the New Testament to a "Mark" are references to the same person and that he is the author of this Gospel, the following has often been related about him.

According to Acts 12:12, he was the son of a fairly affluent woman of Jerusalem whose name was Mary and whose home was a gathering place for the early church. Thus, from young manhood Mark found himself within the inner circle of the Christian fellowship. He must have known the first disciples personally. Mark was also the cousin of Barnabas (Col. 4:10), and when Paul and Barnabas set out on their initial evangelistic enterprise they took Mark with them (Acts 12:25; 13:13). For some unknown reason, when the company came to Perga in Pamphylia (just inland from the southern coast of Turkey), before they began the journey over the Taurus Mountains to Antioch of Pisidia, Mark turned back and went home to Jerusalem (Acts 13:13). Later, when Paul proposed that they " 'return and visit the brethren in every city' " where they had " 'proclaimed the word of the Lord,' " Barnabas wanted to take John Mark with them (Acts 15:37). "But Paul thought best not to take with them one who had withdrawn from them in Pamphylia and had not gone with them to the work. And there arose a sharp contention, so that they separated from each other; Barnabas took Mark with him and sailed away to Cyprus, but Paul chose Silas and departed, being commended by the brethren to the grace of the Lord." (Acts 15:36–41)

We hear nothing more about "Mark" in the New Testament for about ten or fifteen years, and when we do meet him again he is in a surprising place with an unexpected person. From his prison (or "house arrest") in Rome, in the early 60s (or perhaps from a jail in Ephesus about 54–55 A.D.), Paul writes a letter to the church in Colossae; and in his closing remarks he makes this statement: "Aristarchus my fellow prisoner greets you, and Mark the cousin of Barnabas (concerning whom you have received instructions—if he comes to you, receive him), and Jesus who is called Justus. These are the only men of the circumcision among my fellow workers for the kingdom of God, and they have been a comfort to me." (Col. 4:10f.) Obviously a reconciliation has taken place and a deep personal relation has been established. In another prison letter (probably from Rome about 61–63 A.D.), Paul again mentions Mark as a "fellow worker." (Philem. 24)

The last reference to "Mark" in the New Testament is also the most intriguing. In 1 Peter 5:13 we read: "She who is at Babylon, who is likewise chosen, sends you greetings; and so does my son Mark." Babylon is a pseudonym for Rome. A number of New Testament scholars doubt that Peter wrote this letter. Others are convinced, however, that while the "actual composition" of this document "was entrusted to Silvanus (5:12), the missionary companion of Paul (2 Cor. 1:19; 1 Thess. 1:1; 2 Thess. 1:1)," nevertheless "Peter stands in the background as author."[3] *If,* as many believe, this letter was written from Rome (5:13) about 64 A.D., shortly after the beginning of the persecution of Christians by the emperor Nero, and *if* this reference to Mark can be traced back to Peter himself during this time, and, *if* this Mark is the "author" of this document, then we have here an informative insight into the life-experience of the redactor-editor of our gospel.

Based on the presuppositions and the biblical data given above, Professor Paul Minear offers a somewhat speculative but nevertheless revealing summary description of this "John Mark."

> A native of Jerusalem, Mark had at a very early date joined the ranks of the followers of Jesus. He had been associated . . . with the apostolic work of both Peter and Paul. He had visited many churches in all parts of the empire. He had lived through imprisonments; he had seen friends and leaders martyred; he had for several years been at work among Roman Christians who had experienced for at least thirty years the difficulties of following a crucified Lord . . .
> Mark was probably a Jew, well versed in the Law and the prophets, acquainted with the traditions and customs of the Judean homeland and bound by many strong ties to the hope of Israel. He was a Jewish Christian, whose life had been turned upside down by the story of Jesus the Messiah. He had interpreted discipleship as an inescapable call to be a witness and had devoted many years to preaching the gospel in Asia, Achaia, and other Roman provinces. His work had been similar to that of Peter and Paul, and, like theirs, it had carried him into intimate fellowship with Gentile congregations and therefore into the cross fire of opposition from synagogues and even from other Jewish Christians. He had done his best to heal the schism between Christians of left and right wing—a task which was as difficult in Rome as anywhere else.[4]

Such a man, many have said, was the compiler of the Gospel According to Mark.

The Historical Setting of Mark

As with any biblical document, we need to know something of the historical setting in which the Gospel of Mark was produced and the situation of its original recipients in order to understand as accurately and as completely as possible its message for us today. (See above.)

In all probability the Gospel of Mark if not "written" in Rome, found its way to Rome and was used there by Christian congregations (some Jewish, some Gentile, and some mixed) shortly after its composition, some time during the years 65 through 75 A.D. But what does this bare outline statement tell us? A lot, if we supplement it with information from the annals of Roman historians and other New Testament books; and mostly about conflict.

Congregation and Synagogue

In the eighteenth chapter of Acts it is reported that after Paul left Athens he went to Corinth and there found "a Jew named Aquila, a native of Pontus, lately come from Italy with his wife, Priscilla, because Claudius had commanded all the Jews to leave Rome." (Acts 18:2) This expulsion of Jews from Rome (about 49/50 A.D.) is also mentioned by the second-century Roman biographer, Suetonius, who states in his *Lives of the Caesars* that the emperor Claudius (A.D. 41–54) issued this edict because some Jews were "incessantly causing riots with *Chrestus* as the instigator." (*Claudius,* 25) This evidently means two things, and maybe three. (1) The trouble was caused in the Jewish quarter by controversy over whether or not Jesus was the Messiah (*Christos,* in Greek, a concept and a word which Suetonius or his sources did not comprehend and which, therefore, came out in the writing as an individual named *Chrestus*). This indicates that at this time there were Christ-believing Jews in Rome (perhaps Gentile Christians as well) and that there was open conflict between "the congregation" and "the synagogue." Unhappily this continued for years to come. Paul appears to be aware of it when he writes his letter to the Romans (ca. 54–58 A.D.). (See, for example, Rom. 9–11.) (2) As far as the "Roman populace" or the "Gentile world" was concerned at this date the Christians were simply a sect, or a particular branch, of the Jewish religion. Indeed, many of the Jewish Christians themselves sought to remain within the household of Israel and to preserve many of their traditional customs, while attempting to persuade their covenant brothers and sisters of the Messiahship of Jesus. (3) Some biblical scholars suggest that Aquila and Priscilla were Christians before they left Rome and were, in fact, some of the first witnesses to Jesus in the imperial city. (For further mention of this couple in the New Testament, see Acts 18:18, 26; Rom. 16:3; 1 Cor. 16:19; 2 Tim. 4:19.)

It is highly unlikely that Claudius was able to make a clean sweep with his command for expulsion of the Jews (including those who professed Jesus to be *Christos*). Although many were undoubtedly driven out of the city, some must have been able to remain, and some quickly returned. If the sixteenth chapter (the postscript) of Paul's letter to the Romans is a part of the original document, we have here the names of over twenty-five Christians, some of them Jewish (e.g., vss. 7 and 11), representing about five "house churches," or home congregations, who were residents in Rome ca. 54–58 A.D.

Surely Mark was acutely aware of this congregation-synagogue conflict when he compiled his Gospel from the oral and written sources which he had available. Certainly he had this problem in mind when he included the stories which present Jesus so clearly as a Jew of his day, accepting and approving of much in his heritage (synagogue worship, the inner meaning of the old law, the two-fold commandment, the celebration of the feasts, etc.). Relevant also in this positive way were the incidents of opening blind eyes (10:46–52), making the lame to walk (2:1–12), feeding the five thousand (6:30–44), and Jesus' entry into Jerusalem (11:1–10), all of which could have been interpreted as signs of his (redefined) Messiahship (cf. Isa. 35:5–7; 40:11; Zech. 9:9). In this same apologetic or evangelistic category would fall the account of Peter's confession of Jesus as the Christ (8:22–30).

But Mark must have also been sensitive to this Jewish-Christian tension when he used those examples of controversy between Jesus and the Pharisees which demonstrated unequivocally his implicit claim to authority and his break with the official Judaism of his day, as well as the passion narrative which openly declares that the "son of God" (15:39; cf. 1:1), the Messiah (14:61; 15; 1:1) was indeed the man from Nazareth who was crucified. Of special significance, also, in this connection, is the way Mark brackets the story of Jesus' cleansing the temple with his cursing of the fig tree (11:12–25). By so doing Mark is clearly indicating that he intends the two stories to be understood in relation to one another. . . .

> As the tradition is found in Mark, the temple cleansing represents Jesus' prophetic-symbolic act of ending cultic worship within the temple, because it has been abused on the assumption that the temple cult made forgiveness for any kind of behavior automatic, and because the necessary universal worship of God, to be centered in the temple simply had not come about. It is precisely that point that Mark wants to reinforce by combining the traditions of the cursing of the fig tree and the cleansing of the temple.
>
> The fig tree which has not borne its proper fruit, and which therefore has been cursed, is symbolic of the temple which, by Jesus' actions within it, Jesus similarly "cursed."[5]

Gentile Christian and Jewish Christian

A careful reading of Paul's letter to the Romans will reveal that there was conflict not only *between* the congregation and the synagogue, but also *within* the church between Gentile Christian and Jewish Christian.

> Paul's discussion in Romans 14 and 15 shows all too clearly that [they] . . . were at odds with one another. House churches composed of Jews did not extend hospitality to Gentile Christians. Why not? Because these Gentile brothers refused to consider the Sabbath Day holy, according to the commandment of the Law (Deut. 5:12). Furthermore, they refused to observe the dietary commandments of the Law but were in the habit of eating any food, however unclean it might be judged by Scripture. Jewish Christians were therefore impelled by loyalty to God's Word [Old Testament] to consider Gentile Christians unclean and to refuse to eat with them. From the opposite side, these Gentile Christians quite naturally despised and ridiculed their Jewish brothers who held such compunctions about what days were holy and what foods clean. They tried to persuade Jewish disciples to break the Law even before their consciences would permit them to do so. So whenever the two groups met, they fell to wrangling

about food and holy days. Their animosities destroyed the peace and joy which should have been theirs in the Holy Spirit (Rom. 14:17).[6]

In Christian congregations within the city of Rome and within other cities and districts of the empire where there were Christian congregations composed of both Jews and Gentiles this same kind of conflict was likely to occur.

This cleavage was deep and serious. Essentially it was the question of whether or not one must become a Jew in order to become a Christian, or whether or not the church could have diversity within its unity. It was the question of law or freedom, of faction or fellowship. (These questions are obviously not confined to the Roman World of the first century!) Again, Mark was probably keenly aware of this conflict when he composed his Gospel; and, again, in all likelihood, he intended for his first readers/hearers to apply to their immediate situations the significance of Jesus' debates with the scribes and Pharisees, as well as his abrogation of the tradition, his commandment to love, his prescription for "greatness" (" 'Whoever would be great among you must be your servant, and whoever would be first among you must be slave of all.' " 10:43f.), and his warning about causing one of the "little ones" who believe in him to stumble (9:42). And again the lesson of the cleansing of the temple and the cursing of the fig tree is applicable (11:12–25).

A contemporary manifestation of this same kind of conflict-problem may be expressed this way: is it necessary for a modern scientifically-minded person to accept the first century mythological framework of the New Testament (heaven above, hell below, earth between, invaded by angels and demons, etc.) in order to hear and believe the essential meaning of the gospel message?

Church and State

Paul was probably in prison in Rome and awaiting trial (Phil. 1:12–26) when he penned his letter to the church at Philippi around 61–63 A.D. It is possible that Peter was in the city at this time, too. On July 19, 63 A.D. a terrible disaster befell the people of Rome.

> A fire broke out in the shops in a crowded central section. . . . Fanned by strong winds it swept fiercely through the narrow passages and congested streets, killing hundreds and perhaps thousands of the trapped citizens. It consumed temples as well as tenements, and even the emperor's palace was not spared. Of the fourteen wards of the city only four remained untouched; the others were either totally destroyed or badly damaged.
> Nero, the emperor [54–68 A.D.], immediately began rebuilding the devastated city with lavish magnificence along the lines of a new

master plan. But the more vigorously he devoted himself to urban reconstruction, the more his action seemed to substantiate the rumors that he himself had started the fire as the cheapest way to clear the site of his new city. Obviously such rumors did not endear the emperor to the thousands who had lost everything in the holocaust. To shift the blame from his own shoulders, he picked out a group of "foreigners" who were unable to offer resistance: the Christians.[7]

Here is how the Roman historian, Tacitus (ca. 54–118 A.D.), tells it:

> ... But all human efforts, all the lavish gifts of the emperor, and the propitiations of the gods did not banish the sinister belief that the conflagration was the result of an order. Consequently, to get rid of the report, Nero fastened the guilt and inflicted the most exquisite tortures on a class hated for their abominations, called Christians by the populace. Christus, from whom the name had its origin, suffered the extreme penalty during the reign of Tiberius at the hands of one of our procurators, Pontius Pilatus, and a most mischievous superstition thus checked for the moment, again broke out not only in Judaea, the first source of the evil, but even in Rome, where all things hideous and shameful from every part of the world find their centre and become popular. Accordingly, an arrest was first made of all who pleaded guilty; then upon their information, an immense multitude was convicted, not so much of the crime of firing the city, as of hatred against mankind. Mockery of every sort was added to their deaths. Covered with the skins of beasts, they were torn by dogs and perished, or were nailed to crosses, or were doomed to the flames and burnt, to serve as nightly illumination when daylight had expired. Nero offered his gardens for the spectacle, and was exhibiting a show in the circus, while he mingled with the people in the dress of a charioteer or stood aloft on a car. Hence, even for criminals who deserve extreme and exemplary punishment, there arose a feeling of compassion; for it was not, as it seemed, for the public good, but to glut one man's cruelty, that they were being destroyed.[8]

Many New Testament scholars think that it is impossible to pinpoint exactly the historical background of the Gospel of Mark:

> The description of 13:7–8 would fit the destruction brought about by the Jewish rebellion and its quelling by Roman legions in A.D. 66–70. The account of Josephus, a contemporary [Jewish historian], mentions famines and earthquakes as well as national revolts, although such conditions may simply be means of impressing on the reader the utter devastation those events brought with them.[9]

Whatever the particular time and the specific place to which this Gospel was originally addressed, generally speaking it was to Christians in conflict with the civil authorities as well as with "the Synagogue" and with one another (e.g., 13:9–27).

As Mark sifted, selected, and shaped the material he had received from earlier disciples and various congregations, as he recalled the miracles, sayings, parables, and "passion" of Jesus which had been preserved and passed on orally in the church since the inception of the post-resurrection community, he was sensitive to the condition of those for whom he was preparing his Gospel. By choosing and including the accounts of the attitude and action of Herod (6:14–29) and Pilate (15:1–15), he was not simply reporting events. He was also telling the Christians at Rome and elsewhere in the empire that both "the forerunner" and the Master himself had suffered at the hands of this same governmental system. When he recorded the saying of Jesus, " 'Render to Caesar the things that are Caesar's, and to God the things that are God's,' " (12:17) he knew that this would have special meaning for his readers. For those who were so recently and painfully familiar with the cost of discipleship, and who at any moment might be called upon again to confess their faith with their lives, Jesus' invitation in 8:34–9:1 would be both stern warning and strong comfort. All of chapter 13 would have immediate relevance to all Christians caught in the often deadly crunch between the claims of Christ and compulsory allegiance to Caesar about 65–75 A.D., particularly vss. 9–13:

> "But take heed to yourselves; for they will deliver you up to councils; and you will be beaten in synagogues; and you will stand before governors and kings for my sake, to bear testimony before them. And the gospel must first be preached to all nations. And when they bring you up to trial and deliver you up, do not be anxious beforehand what you are to say; but say whatever is given you in that hour, for it is not you who speak, but the Holy Spirit. And brother will deliver up brother to death, and the father his child, and children will rise against parents, and have them put to death; and you will be hated by all for my name's sake. But he who endures to the end will be saved." (Cf. also 10:28–31.)

The story of Peter's denial of Jesus (14:53–72) and the knowledge of his subsequent restoration to the fellowship would speak redemptively to those individuals who had not been able to stand the test (is Jesus Lord or is Caesar Lord?) and had, therefore, replied to their interrogators, " 'I do not know this man of whom you speak,' " (14:71) as well as to congregations that had been riddled by betrayals.

The narrative which is concerned with only the last single day in the life of Jesus (14:17–15:39) is at the same time the longest unbroken episode in the book. If we add to this the series of events prior to the crucifixion—from Jesus' entry into Jerusalem, through the Last Supper, the arrest, and the trials —plus the incident of the empty tomb, we have encompassed the last week and almost two thirds (11–16) of the content of this entire document. This must indicate that Mark was convinced that the crucial significance of Jesus was to be communicated primarily through this section of his story.

The message could not be missed by Mark's readers and hearers wherever they were. The Living One who is with them, offering them life in the midst of conflict, crisis, and death, is the same One who was pursued, persecuted, and killed. The only life he has to give, therefore, is life on the yonder side of the cross; and his invitation is "Come follow me."

Questions for Further Reflection and Discussion

Was the hostility between church and synagogue in the first century inevitable? What are the possibilities, if any, for further reconciliation between Christians and Jews today? Were the divisions within the Christian community in Rome "necessary"? Are denominational groupings today based on fundamentally different understandings of the Gospel? Do you think there are any essential elements of the faith on which all Christians can agree? Are there any "non-essentials" in denominational beliefs or practices which you think denominations should be willing to give up in order to attain greater Christian unity? How do Jesus' proclamation and demonstration that "the kingdom of God is at hand," his crucifixion and resurrection, and his call to take up the cross relate to the problem of factions within the Christian fellowship? Is there any kind of church-state conflict within the world today? Within the United States? Do our state or federal governments express hostility toward the church? Does our constitution promote or hinder religion? Is the freedom of religion currently being fostered or denied in our country? How? Is it possible to be both a faithful participant in the kingdom of God and a responsible citizen of the state? How? Are the two the same?

Conflict in Contemporary Culture

Most of the issues have been raised, directly or indirectly, in the sections above. Only a brief attempt at a translation of meaning will be offered here. To put it simply, the Gospel of Mark proclaims that God himself has openly declared and demonstrated that this world is his, and that he is active in it, bringing people out of darkness into light, out of bondage into freedom, out of sin into salvation, out of death into life. He did this "once and for all" in and through the words and the deeds, the crucifixion and the resurrection of Jesus. He does it today in a variety of ways through Christ who is yet alive and at work within the world. But even as he was victor, and liberator, and healer, and forgiver, and giver of life back then *only as he went through Gethsemane to Golgotha as the obedient Son* (1:1; 14:36; 15:39), so is he today, through all other sons and daughters who obediently take up the cross and follow him.

Even as the conflict, though joined, decided, and won in him, continued in the age of the author of this Gospel, so it does today. The eschatalogical element in the teaching of Jesus (8:38–9:1; 13:26) and in the life of the church must not be ignored or even diminished. "The kingdom of God is at hand," but it is yet to be consummated. The Son of man has come (8:31), but he is ever yet the Coming One (8:38; 13:26). For the Christian today this means four things: (1) The world and humankind, all culture and every aspect of contemporary humanity (art, science, business, technology, government, religion) stand under, are responsible to, and are judged by God. It is God (in Christ) who both questions and affirms persons and their culture. (2) The forces of evil still challenge the authority of God in innumerable ways. Sin is still potent and active through people. We still refuse to love God and our brothers and sisters as ourselves. Unwilling to acknowledge our responsibility to God and our neighbor, we still enslave other persons in poverty and ignorance, kill them with bombs and prejudice, cripple them with injustice and suppression, either actively or apathetically by remaining aloof and uninvolved. (3) Christians in these conflicts in contemporary culture are called to acknowledge God's authoritative rule in the world and to allow the saving power of Christ to be expressed through the whole of their lives. They are to find out where and how the reign of God is being realized in the world, celebrate it, and participate in it. They are to follow Jesus as liberator and lifegiver. They know this will not be easy or simple. They are aware that it will be difficult and complex. (4) Whoever repents and believes in the Gospel, whoever confesses irresponsibility and acknowledges that this is God's world by actively participating in his saving, liberating, and life-giving rule, *can do so with confidence.* These people can be sure that the redemptive power of God, by whomever and however it is expressed (Mark 9:38–40), is ultimately effective, even when, indeed precisely when, it appears to be most ineffectual. For the person of faith knows that the power of God is the cross of Christ (1 Cor. 1:17–25)!

Interpretive reflections on representative passages in Mark's Gospel

Employing those methodologies discussed in Parts I and II, and incorporating those insights into the background of the Gospel of Mark reflected in the preceding essay, let us come now to an exploration of the meanings of individual and representative passages in this early Christian profession of faith.

The Beginning of the Good News
Mark 1:1–20

The *introduction* to the entire presentation of Mark's understanding of Jesus consists of five main sections: (1) the title of the book (1:1); (2) the role of John the Baptist (1:2–8); (3) the baptism and temptation of Jesus (1:9–13); (4) the preaching of Jesus (1:14–15); (5) the calling of the first disciples (1:16–20).

The Title of the Book (1:1)

"The beginning of the gospel of Jesus Christ, the Son of God." This opening statement, along with each individual part of it, is packed with vital significance. As we approach it let us notice initially its grammatical character. It is not a full sentence because it does not have a verb. It appears to be a title indicating the subject of the writing. It is, therefore, somewhat analogous to "The Origin and Development of the Concept of Liberty" or "The Annual Report of the Board of World Missions."

But to what exactly does Mark's title refer? Obviously to "the beginning." But what *is* "the beginning." Some students of Mark say that here he intends to designate the ministry of John the Baptist (1:2–8) and thereby to connect it with the proclamation and the action of Jesus (1:14f.). This interpretation is certainly possible. Undoubtedly, by the use of the quotations from the Old Testament prophets (vss. 2–3), the appearance, preaching, and baptism of John (vss. 4–8), and the order of events (vss. 4–15), Mark is saying that the preparation in which John engaged is the first chapter of the story which finds its fulfillment in Jesus. Sequentially Jesus follows John, but the "good news" actually begins with "the forerunner." This seems to be clearly implied in Mark's composition of verses 2–15. But this understanding of the passage is possible without any reference to verse 1. Indeed, no other narrative in this document is preceded by a title or headed with a thematic statement.[10]

For these reasons many commentators do not connect verse 1 immediately and solely with verses 2–8 (the ministry of John). They see it rather as standing alone and read it as *the title of the whole book.* If this is the case, then Mark is saying that *all* of that which he presents in this document is *"the beginning of the Gospel of Jesus Christ, the Son of God."* And what does Mark present? Both the event of Jesus and the word about Jesus, God's action in Jesus and the believer's witness to Jesus. The two are indivisible. But if, as his title states, Mark is telling of the *beginning* of the Gospel (might we say *only* the beginning?) what, when, and where is "the continuing"? Is it not the authoritative, liberating, and life-giving action of Jesus within both the church and the world? Is it not the continuing communication of this good news by all those who respond, through both their words and their deeds, at any time and in any place? This brings us to the second part of the title: "the gospel of Jesus Christ."

The Greek word *euanggelion,* which in the New Testament is translated *gospel,* originally meant "the reward of good tidings."[11] Later it signified the "good news" itself. The *euanggelion* is not a casual mention of some insignificant happening, not a bit of idle chatter passed over the back fence. Rather it is a historic announcement of life-changing import read with fitting ceremony by the King's representative or called aloud by the royal crier in the city square. And if, for example, the gospel is the word that the city and all its inhabitants have been rescued from military seige, liberated from their captors, or saved from death, then it is great news indeed! It radically alters the corporate and individual existence of the people who hear it.

It is the beginning of this kind of *euanggelion* which Mark sets forth in and through his Gospel. It is "the gospel of Jesus Christ." To be sure, its meaning for all those to whom it is addressed can be fully known only upon reading the whole of Mark's tract. Therefore we should not attempt to state *conclusively* at the outset its central significance. (But see above the discussion of three major themes and the essay, "Christ and Conflict.") We must ask this question again at the end of our study. However, merely on the basis of this initial reference we may say three things in general. In one sense the gospel is *God's* announcement of the salvation of humanity in and through the words and deeds of Jesus. In a second and particular sense it is Jesus' own declaration that " 'the kingdom of God is at hand.' " (1:15) In a third and special sense it is the proclamation of Mark (and other witnesses in every generation —early and late) of the meaning of Jesus for people's salvation, the good news *about* Jesus. It is probably this last connotation which Mark primarily intended when he used the phrase "the gospel of Jesus Christ."

Jesus is the Greek form of the Hebrew name Joshua, (or "the Lord saves"), and Christ (Greek *Christos*) is the translation of Messiah. By the time Mark wrote his Gospel, "Jesus Christ" was the personal name commonly used by Christians to designate the "Savior" and "Lord" within the Hellenistic/Roman world and the Jewish/Gentile church (cf. above, "Titles for Jesus Are Telling").

The last part of the title, "Son of God," like the word gospel, can accurately be defined only as we read through Mark's entire proclamation of Jesus. What he means by the term "Son of God" is *all* that he says in his Gospel *about* Jesus. General tentative suggestions may, however, be appropriate. Commenting on this verse, Vincent Taylor remarks: "A supernatural being is described, but not with the precision of Phil. ii. 6 or Lk. i. 35."[12] Other "sons" of God were known and worshiped in the Greco-Roman world. For example, the mythical figure of Heracles was believed to be one of these "saviors" and "helpers of humankind," and he was the object of utmost devotion for some people. "The concept [of] 'Son of God' ... represented the very highest attainment of popular pagan religion."[13] It is possible that the early Christians outside Palestine took this designation from their cultural environment and filled it with new meaning. "In the same way the present-day church in ... India chooses terms already full of deep religious significance and then proceeds to give them their fullest possible meaning in connection with Christ, God, or the Holy Spirit."[14]

From the first-century Jewish Christian perspective, the perspective from which Mark probably wrote his Gospel, it is likely that the meaning of this title "Son of God" would be that of "functional" sonship. What *is* a son? Naturally a son is the biological offspring of parents. But this obviously is not what Jesus is in relation to God. In fact, there are many male children who are born into the world who are *not truly sons* of their fathers. The parent does not know or love the child nor does the child know or love the parent. At the same time, even in some families today, the oldest son is really "son" only, or primarily, insofar as he is the *representative* of the father. This was particularly true in the first century A.D. In obedience to the father the son did the father's will (14:36; cf. 3:34–35). He spoke for the father and acted on the father's behalf. He conducted the father's business and accomplished the tasks to which he was commissioned by the father (cf. 1:38). Many people knew the father only through his *agent,* his son. It was perhaps this functional meaning of sonship which Mark had in mind fundamentally when he applied the title "Son of God" to Jesus (cf. 3:11; 5:7; 15:39; 1:11; 9:7; 14:61). But more about Jesus as the "Son of God" in the comments on his baptism below.

The Role of John the Baptist (1:2–8)

Two quotations (1:2b, 3) from the Old Testament are used to introduce interpretively the role of John the Baptist in relation to Jesus. The first (1:2b) is not from the prophet Isaiah as indicated in 1:2a. It is rather a combination of Exodus 23:20a and Malachi 3:1. It may have been taken from a collection of "Messianic proofs" employed by early preachers to demonstrate that he who was crucified was the fulfillment of the hope and expectation of Israel. The second Old Testament quotation (1:3) is from Isaiah 40:3. Both of these Old Testament references, together with the account of John's appearance, preaching, and baptism (1:4–8), assert that the *prophetic preparation* which was necessary just prior to the coming of him who, as both Judge (Mal. 3:1–5) and Deliverer (Isaiah 40:1–11) would usher in the New Age, did in fact occur.

And what is the nature of this prophetic preparation, which though it precedes the actual event of salvation is nevertheless an integral part of it? It is a twofold proclamation (1:4, 7). On the one hand it is the preaching of a "baptism of repentance for the forgiveness of sins." (1:4) It is the call for a ritual washing which openly signifies a radical change from an attitude of opposition to one of receptivity, a deliberate *turning* from the old (present) mode of being without God and against one's fellowpersons (cf. Rom. 1:18–32) to the possibility of existence with God and for the neighbor. Such a baptism, including confession (1:5), not only publicly symbolizes but also effectively results in a real cleansing, a pardoning of offenses, a *readiness* for participation in that kingdom which is soon to be established. On the other hand it is the preaching (1:7–8) of that Mightier One who is immediately coming, who will bring in the reign of God, and who will baptize with the Holy Spirit, thereby imparting the permanent breath of God, the sustaining power of Life.

One more important implication of John's ministry must be noted. The fact that multitudes of Jews were flocking to this Elijah in the wilderness (cf. 1:5–6; 2 Kings 1:8; Mal. 3:1; 4:5f.), listening to him and accepting his baptism, indicates something of the excited hope, the frenzied expectation which was rampant among the Jews at this time. They were impatiently waiting, standing on their tiptoes, craning their necks, and looking for the Messiah, the royal representative of God who would defeat his and their enemies and establish his realm of peace and security, righteousness and prosperity; or the mythical "Son of man" who would come down from heaven to exercise judgment as the agent of the Almighty (cf. Dan. 7:13; 1 Enoch 46:1, 3; 48:2f.; 51:3; 62:2, 6; 69:27f.). But no one was anticipating a cruicified Christ.

The Baptism and Temptation of Jesus (1:9–13)

The two-sided experience of Jesus' baptism/temptation, as Mark employs the tradition, has deep and far-reaching symbolic connotation. (1) By accepting the baptism of John with the common people, he who is to announce and demonstrate the fulfillment of their hopes (in an unexpected way), *identifies* with them as one of them. Jesus does not stand aloof from those who, aware of their sin, repent and seek forgiveness. These are his kind of people! And it is precisely within their midst that he receives *confirmation of this calling with authority and power to fulfill it.* (2) The rending of the heavens and the descending of the Spirit symbolize *God's certification* of this one as his anointed (appointed) representative (cf. 1 Sam. 16:13; Isa. 61:1), his legitimate agent. They therefore signify also Jesus' embodiment of God's authority (cf. 1:22; 13:31) and power (eg., 1:23–28; 3:22–27). The heavens represent the royal abode of Deity and his sovereign Being (cf. Matt. 4:17). The Spirit of God is literally his breath. Symbolically it is his life and strength. The newly baptized Christian in Rome during the first century (or in any place at any time) who believes that in this sacrament she or he receives the Holy Spirit in a special way (cf. Acts 2:38) will find immediate relevance in the baptism of Jesus.

The metaphorical expression "like a dove" is derived from Jewish imagery. It probably denotes the creating and ordering action of God. It recalls the picture in Genesis 1:2. With this verse in mind, Ben Zoma, a younger rabbinic contemporary of the early disciples wrote: " 'I was considering the space between the upper waters and the lower waters . . . and the Spirit of God was brooding on the face of the waters like a dove broods over her young but does not touch them.' "[15]

The implication that Jesus now possesses and uses this divine creative and order-producing power is remarkable. In inaugurating the kingdom of God, Jesus accomplishes a *re-creation,* a restoration of right order, in which the forces of chaos (demons, evil, disease) are subdued and kept under control. (3) The "voice from heaven" is addressed to Jesus. It therefore denotes the *assurance,* or confirmation, which Jesus receives (and the claim which the evangelist here makes) that he is in fact the appointed "Son of God," the representative of the Father. It also further defines the nature of this sonship. What "the voice" says is a combination of two short excerpts from the Old Testament: Psalm 2:7 and Isaiah 42:1. (It also echoes other Old Testament passages: Gen. 22:2; Isa. 44:2; 62:4.)[16] In the New Testament, brief quotations from the Old Testament are often used to recall and apply the meaning of the whole passage from which they are taken. Psalm 2 is about the mighty conquering king. Isaiah 42 is about the obedient servant of the Lord. Together they make the unique and provocative assertion that Jesus is *the strong deliverer* precisely as he is the *humble slave* of God who gives his life for others. (The Servant also appears in Isaiah 49:1-6; 50:4-11; 52:13-53:12; cf. Mark 10:45.)

(4) The version of Jesus' temptation which Mark uses in writing his Gospel (1:12f.; cf. Matt. 4:1-11; Luke 4:1-13) is very brief. It is possible that he presupposes a knowledge of the accounts found in Matthew and Luke. In both of these the primary point seems to be that Jesus is tempted not to respond to his calling at all, or to fulfill his redemptive role some other way. In Mark the fundamental idea appears to be that this same Spirit which possessed him and which he was given at his baptism now ("immediately") forces him straight into the stronghold of the Enemy to do battle with him. But this is not only the outset of this conflict; it is also a characterization of Jesus' whole life. The phrase "forty days" means "a long time." It reminds us of the "forty years" that Israel wandered in the wilderness (Exod. 16:35, etc.), a period of preparation and testing; the "forty days and forty nights" Moses spent with God on the mountain, neither eating nor drinking, as he wrote the Ten Commandments on the two tablets of stone—a time and an act of covenant mediation (Exod. 34:27f.); the "forty days and forty nights" of Elijah's journey to Horeb (1 Kings 19:8), a pilgrimage made in the strength of God. The association of wilderness, wild beast, and the domain of Satan would come to mind for readers familiar with Isaiah 34:8-17 and intertestamental Jewish literature such as The Testament of the Twelve Patriarchs (Naphthali 8, Issachar 7, Benjamin 5).

The Preaching of Jesus (1:14-15)

This is a summary statement. The work of "The Preparer" is completed. The main character of the drama now holds the center of the stage. The essential theme, which he will communicate through all that he says and does, is now delivered in capsule form, and it is "the gospel of God." *The time is fulfilled.* That God-appointed period of preparation, waiting, and expectation is concluded. (Compare Ezek. 7:12; Dan. 12:4, 9; Zeph. 1:12; Gal. 4:4; Eph. 1:10; Matt. 26:18; Luke 21:8 for the concept of the divinely determined "Time" or *kairos*.) The end of the old aeon, the old mode of existence has come. *The kingdom of God is at hand.* The sovereign rule, the authoritative reign of God is very near. It is quickly coming. In fact, its presence is anticipated by this very proclamation and by the one who makes it. This announcement is good news. And it demands decision. You cannot earn the kingdom. You cannot build it. It does not evolve. It is totally God's being and doing. He offers it as gift (cf. Luke 12:32). It means openness to the

King's command, radical and momentary obedience. *Repent and believe in the Gospel.* Thus Jesus and Mark proclaim and offer the "good news."

Note: One of the most difficult questions of New Testament study is whether Jesus thought and preached that the kingdom of God was future, or present, or both. The position taken here is that Jesus proclaimed the kingdom as future (1:15; 9:1; 14:25), while, in effect, realizing it in the present through his words and deeds (e.g., 1:21–28, 29–45; 2:1–3:6; 3:22–27; cf. Matt. 11:1–6; Luke 7:18–23). For Mark also the *full actualization* of the kingdom is still future (13). But it has already begun; it has been inaugurated and established in and through Jesus. Mark's Roman readers in the midst of their conflicts would understand this view clearly and appreciate it keenly. And, of course, Mark's presentation of the Gospel was influenced by the situation of those to whom he addressed it.

Perhaps the most important facts about the kingdom which readers or hearers of Mark's Gospel must remember in order to understand it and receive it are the following: It is not a horizontal realm. It is a vertical relation. It is not a political, or social, or even an ethical sphere of existence which either naturally evolves or is produced by humans. It is God's authoritative Being, Ruling, and Acting, which people gratefully are to acknowledge and gladly accept, and which has ethical consequences (individual and corporate) for those who thus participate in it. It means momentary openness to God's command and immediate obedience to his will. It is a constant call to decision in the here and now. It is, therefore, life continually under God's question and God's affirmation, his judgment and his grace.

The Calling of the First Disciples (1:16–20)

Immediately after announcing the kingdom of God, which is near at hand and quickly coming, Jesus calls disciples to follow him into it and to share in the heralding of it. We do not know for sure whether these men had seen Jesus and heard his message before or not. Possibly they had. But for his purpose Mark is not interested in reporting the full "factual" details of what actually happened. He may not have even known them. He rather employs this brief episode, which was part of the common tradition widely circulated and used in the preaching and teaching of the church, to illustrate two central points in the proclamation of Jesus which he has summarized in the preceding verse: "repent and believe."[17] We might translate these words "turn and trust." When they are put into action they become "leave and follow." This is exactly what these fishermen did. "And immediately they left their nets and followed him." (1:18, 20) They make a clean break with their old and customary way of life with all its security and move out in faith following Jesus into the new and unknown mode of being with all its insecurity. As the story stands, all that Jesus promises them is to make them become fishers of men.

He has cast his net and he has caught them for the kingdom. He will teach them how to do the same for others. They also are to become proclaimers of his gospel.

It convicted and encouraged and quickened the church in the Roman world to read or hear again that Christ's church was begun in response to his call to discipleship, his commission to evangelize, and his companionship on the way.

Jesus' Teaching: Exorcising Demons, Healing Diseases, and Preaching the Gospel
Mark 1:21–45

Most of the background information necessary for an adequate understanding of Mark 1:21–45 has been given in the preceding essay *Christ and Conflict* under the headings "Conflict in the Cosmos" and "Conflict in Palestine." Therefore, in this interpretive reflection we will concentrate upon the interpretation of this passage within the total purpose of Mark (to proclaim Jesus as God's Representative, Servant Son, and Victor over the forces of evil, sin, and death) and its possible translation into categories of our contemporary life.

Jesus' Teaching: New, Authoritative, and Powerful (1:21–28)

Through his use of this "miracle-story" Mark apparently intends to say three things about the teaching of Jesus, and, therefore, implicitly about Jesus himself. The last half of verse 27 serves as a summary: " 'What is this? A *new* teaching! With authority he commands even the unclean spirits, and *they obey him.*' " (Author's emphasis.)

Obviously the first question we must ask and seek to answer is this: *what* did Jesus teach that was new, authoritative, and powerful? Mark does not tell us outright. But we are not left without some fairly clear indications. One hint is found in verse 24. The demon cries out: "What is it between you and us, Jesus of Nazareth? You have come to destroy us! [There was no question mark in the original Greek manuscripts and this sentence should probably be read as an exclamatory statement.] I know who you are, the Holy One of God." (Author's translation.) What teaching would precipitate this violent reaction? Nothing less than the announcement we have already heard in 1:15: " 'The time is fulfilled, and the kingdom of God is at hand.' " The imminent realization of the sovereign rule of God means the imminent termination of the counterfeit reign of the Usurper. The "unclean spirit" comprehends quite clearly the inevitable implication of Jesus' word. He knows who Jesus is—the One appointed by God not only to speak but also to personify his message. He recognizes that as such Jesus is the ultimate threat to his very existence. He, therefore, furiously *resists* (cf. vs. 26).

Let us try a translation. Jesus is the Son (representative) of God, who offers liberation and life. The demon is agent (representative) of the Devil who symbolizes bondage and death. Whenever, wherever, and however the two meet, conflict occurs. Question to Mark's readers and hearers: on which side do you stand?

When the people in the synagogue hear Jesus and observe the consequences of his word they are *amazed.* For his teaching is new, authoritative, and powerful. How is it *new?* What makes it different from all other instruction they had received in that place? The unique quality of Jesus' teaching was that it got results. It changed things. Look what happened! A man who was possessed by an evil force, and thereby separated from God and neighbor, is set free and restored to communion and fellowship. Nothing any other rabbi had expounded from that pulpit had ever had that kind of effect. The reason was that Jesus "taught them as one who had *authority,* and not as the scribes." (Vs. 22, author's emphasis) The professional interpreters of God's Law depended upon the insights and the applications of others ("the tradition of the elders"—7:5; cf. 7:8). Jesus spoke directly, independently, confidently. This was audacious. It was presumptive. It was prophetic. It had the sound of "Thus says the LORD" (cf. Amos 1:3ff.). And like that ancient word of God, which it was believed, had long been silent (cf. Ps. 74:9; 1 Macc. 4:46; 9:27; 14:41) it did not return "empty" but rather "accomplished" that which was purposed, and "prospered" in the thing for which it was sent (Isa. 55:11). In this sense it was dynamic. In this way it was *powerful.* It was liberating (Exod. 5:1; 6:10; 8:1, *et al.*) and *re-creating* (Gen. 1:1—2:3).

Thus by retelling this short drama, through which the early church had professed its comprehension of the character of Jesus' teaching, Mark preached the gospel. For Christians in the Roman world who were confined and crippled it was good to hear again that Jesus' new, authoritative, and powerful word was freeing and healing and that it was Jesus himself through whom this word was effective in their lives. Nor, because they knew the end of the story as well as the beginning, would they forget that the One who both spoke and enacted this word was the One who was crucified and raised from the dead. For others, within and without the church, this word and its freeing and healing result would pose a crucial question: by *whose* authority and power is this new teaching done?

Jesus' Healing: Preservative, Restorative, and Forgiving (1:29–45)

The remaining gospel material in chapter 1 (with the exception of the interlude in verses 35–39 which concludes by pointing up Jesus' preaching) is mostly about Jesus' ministry of healing. (Further exorcisms are mentioned in verse 34.) In the terse account of the healing of Peter's mother-in-law (1:29–31) the reader's attention is focused on the therapeutic action of Jesus which results in the preservation of endangered life and the restoration of the person from a state of incapacity to a meaningful role of service. The fact that this preservation and restoration occur in the home of disciples is significant. As Paul Minear comments: "In similar homes in Rome, disciples would be conscious of the Lord's abiding presence. They would tell him of 'her.' And this Lord would come, would take 'her' by the hand and would lift 'her' up. Then she would be healed and, since she might not have been a believer, would now become one who 'served.' "[18] Does Christ still "heal" like this? If so, in what ways? Through whom?

The incident of the cleansing of the leper (1:40–45) emphasizes the restorative effect and introduces the forgiving quality of Jesus' healing action (which becomes more explicit in the next section). Notice how the deed and word of Jesus are inseparable (vs. 41).

The dreaded disease of leprosy was thought to be more than a mere physical ailment. For the Jews in Jesus' day it was an indication also of sinful contamination. And because it was believed to be a highly contagious infection, the poor leper was both a social and religious outcast. He was forbidden all the normal relations that make existence human. He was separated from synagogue and Temple and thereby cut out of the sphere of God's presence, the realm of true Life. In response to the trustful entreaty of this wretched untouchable (1:40), Jesus, moved with pity, "stretched out his hand and *touched* him." (1:41) In so doing Jesus "took upon himself the dreaded contamination."[19] He *commanded,* " 'be clean.' And immediately the leprosy left him." (1:42) The results were restoration to real humanity and termination of deadly alienation (1:44).

Early Reactions to Jesus
Mark 2:1–3:6

This passage from Mark's Gospel has also been dealt with rather extensively in the section titled "Conflict in Palestine." There it was suggested that three definitive traits of Jesus are disclosed by Mark through his use of this collection of individual units of proclamatory and didactic material. These characteristics of Jesus are: (1) his attitude of *authority;* (2) his attitude of open *receptivity;* (3) his attitude of *freedom* from legal tradition. It will be appropriate and perhaps helpful to reread this section and keep it in mind as we seek to further comprehend the significance of the incidents recorded in 2:1–3:6.

As Mark wrote his Gospel he selected and included certain stories about Jesus which had been formulated, preserved, and passed on within circles of believers for special purposes. Some were used for preaching, some for teaching; some were used in worship services. Others served primarily in ethical exhortation. Others aided in the explanation of situations which existed in the early church. The stories recorded in Mark 2:1–3:6 would help readers and hearers understand why there was conflict between the congregation and the synagogue and between Gentile Christians and Jewish Christians in the Roman Empire of the first century A.D. (See the section above titled "Conflict in Rome.")

Some of the short narratives about Jesus, which were first fashioned during the period of "oral transmission" (ca. 33–50 A.D.) and later written down in the manuscripts, are called paradigms or pronouncement stories. Their main concern is to communicate a saying of Jesus. Most of the episodes which Mark employs in 2:1–3:6 fall generally into this category. In the story of "The Roof Paralytic" (2:1–12), which is probably a combination of a miracle story and a paradigm, the words of Jesus stand out: " 'My son, your sins are forgiven,' " (2:5*b*) " ' "Rise, take up your pallet and walk." ' " (2:9*b*; cf. vs. 11) "The Call of Levi and Jesus' Eating with Sinners" (2:13–17, especially vss. 15–17) lead up to the statement, " 'Those who are well have no need of a physician, but those who are sick; I came not to call the righteous, but sinners.' " (2:17) The most prominent parts of the "The Question about Fasting" (2:18–20) and the analogies of "Patches and Wineskins" (2:21f.) are the sayings of Jesus about the presence of "The Bridegroom" (2:19f.) and the problem of "The Old and the New" (2:21f.). The climax of the episode of "Plucking Grain on the Sabbath" (2:23–28) is reached when Jesus asserts: " 'The sabbath was made for man, not man for the sabbath.' " (2:27*a*) In the incident of "Healing the Man with the Withered Hand" (3:1–6) the *action* of Jesus is subordinate to his *word*: " 'Is it lawful on the sabbath to do good or to do harm, to save life or to kill?' " (3:4)

If, when we study Mark and the other Gospels, we are aware that we are reading pronouncement stories (or other forms such as miracle stories [e.g., 1:23–28]; parables [e.g., 4:26–29]; shorter sayings [e.g., 4:21–25], etc.), we will know where to center our attention for interpretation.

Faith and Expectation

In the story of "The Healing of the Paralytic" (2:1–12) we are told that this action of Jesus is preceded by his preaching of "the word." (2:2) What was this word, which is here not further defined? It must have been the fullness of that original announcement, " 'The kingdom of God is at hand.' " (1:15) It was the word which was being demonstrated in his exorcisms and healings. To this word and this action five men respond in faith and expectation (2:3–5).

This story tells us nothing about these men except what they did. That is all that is important. The socio-economic background from which they come, the particular religious group to which they belong (if any), whether they are good or bad—none of these considerations are of any consequence. They were probably simply a part of the crowd (2:2). As such they were just ordinary people. But they were convinced that the word which they had heard was true and the One who had spoken it had power to heal. Certainly the man on the stretcher was willing to trust himself to Jesus, to allow Jesus to do to and for him whatever he could and would. It seems that the other four shared this *faith* (2:5). They do not hesitate to go to great trouble to get the paralytic into the presence of Jesus. They let nothing prevent them from placing this man before the One whom they believe can do for him that which he most desperately needs—to be made mobile, well, and whole. They are urgently expectant. Where can faith like this be found today? In whom or in what is it placed and why?

Amazement and Praise

After Jesus cured the paralytic "he rose, and immediately took up the pallet and went out before them all; so that they were all amazed and glorified God, saying, 'We never saw anything like this!' " (2:12) As this text now stands in Mark it reads as if the "all" includes the scribes (cf. vss. 6f.). Matthew identifies this group with the "crowds." (Matt. 9:8) If Mark's version of this story intends to say that the scribes also were amazed and praised God in response to Jesus' restorative declaration-deed (2:5, 9–11) then a radical change occurred in their attitude (cf. vss. 6f.). And if "the scribes" in this story are to be associated with "the scribes of the Pharisees" in the paradigm of "Jesus' Eating with Sinners" (2:15–17), then this change was not permanent. If we understand, however, that we are dealing here with two separate units of tradition about Jesus, each preserved and used in the church for a special purpose, then there is no problem and no explanation is necessary. The story of the healing of the paralytic would speak directly to a situation of controversy in which the authority and power of Jesus to forgive sins needed to be reasserted. The incident of Jesus' eating with sinners would be instructive for congregations where hostility between Jewish and Gentile Christians existed (cf. Acts 11:3; Gal. 2:12; and the section above, "Conflict in Rome"). In either case a large number of people are said to have reacted with amazement and praise when they saw the man who had been unable to move get up and walk away. The Greek verb which is translated "were amazed" is very strong. It means literally "to be beside oneself." These people were "overcome"; they were "awe-struck." The Greek verb behind "glorified" is *doxadzein* from which we get our word "doxology." It means to acknowledge God for who he is, to render due tribute to him, to worship him. In effect these people were saying yes to Jesus as the authentic representative of God. For this we are reluctant to criticize them. Is not Mark saying, "Look! They saw and believed. Do you?" Perhaps. But we must not fail to notice that their amazement and praise were in response to the spectacular. This is to be contrasted to the faith and expectation of the paralytic and his bearers, exercised simply on the basis of Jesus' word (2:2) and prior to any overwhelming "miracle."

Question and Rejection

When Jesus says to the paralytic, " 'My son, your sins are forgiven,' " some of the scribes question "in their hearts, 'Why does this man speak thus? It is blasphemy! Who can forgive sins but God alone?' " (2:6f.) When the scribes of the Pharisees see Jesus eating with sinners and tax collectors, they ask his disciples, "Why?" (2:16) When John's disciples and the Pharisees are fasting but Jesus' disciples are not, people ask Jesus "Why not?" (2:18) When Jesus allows his disciples to pick and eat corn on the sabbath, the Pharisees ask " 'Why are they doing what is not lawful?' " (2:24) Finally after Jesus heals the man with the withered hand on the sabbath the Pharisees go out and immediately hold counsel with the Herodians (allies of the Roman puppet king) "how to destroy him." (3:6) One cannot blame the scribes, the Pharisees, and others for questioning Jesus seriously. The Greek word *dialogidzomai* (2:6) means to debate within one's self, to weigh the evidence pro and con within one's mind and heart. At the outset, at least, this questioning was an honest struggle. And we can understand it. For, after all, to pronounce forgiveness of sin is to assume divine prerogative. To eat with sinners is to accept the unacceptable. To refrain from an appointed fast is to disregard a spiritual exercise symbolic of devotion and humility. To pick corn and heal on the sabbath is to breach (the current interpretation of) the sacred code. No wonder they questioned! But they also quickly answered. The system is closed. There is no opening for a new entry of God. Especially not if his agent does not fit the predetermined pattern, if he will not conform to the established status quo. Holy law and order must take precedence over people. Otherwise think of the possible implications! Therefore this presumptive nonconformist tradition-breaker must be stopped!

People Misunderstand Jesus—Demons Do Not!
Mark 3:7–35

In a general sense our study of this section of Mark is a continuation of our last interpretive reflection. For here, too, we are concerned primarily with reactions to Jesus. However, there is a difference. Whereas in 2:1–3:6 a variety of attitudes toward Jesus are portrayed (at least three), in 3:7–35 all of the groups, as Mark represents them, with the single and remarkable exception of the "unclean spirits" in 3:11f., share a basic and common characteristic: they misunderstand Jesus.

It was never the Gospel writer's purpose simply to report past events. He was always addressing the present congregation with both question and affirmation. If we, therefore, are to read Mark aright we must read asking, "What would this say to me, to us, right now? Where and how could we see ourselves in the pictures Mark has drawn?"

Discussion of background concepts pertinent to this passage and suggestions for current translation of its meaning (specifically the references to the demons in 3:11f., 22–27) may be found above in the thematic essay, *Christ and Conflict,* under the heading "Conflict in the Cosmos."

The Multitude (3:7–10)

The masses respond to Jesus as if he were merely a wonder worker, only a faith healer. As his reputation as a curer of ills spreads, large numbers of those who suffer from ailments throng to him, just to touch him, in order to be healed.

Undoubtedly Mark *is* proclaiming that Jesus is the Great Physician, particularly if we remember that for many in the first century *sickness signified sin.* But he is also showing the superficial level on which the multitude reacted to Jesus and how they therefore misunderstood him. They appear to be concerned almost solely with getting what they can out of him. We are not told that they join him as disciples. They follow him for a reason other than obedience to his word. (Notice the distinction made between the disciples and the multitude in 3:7f.) The crowds are attracted by his teaching (10:1). They are willing to listen to him (cf. 4:1). But their overriding desire is to profit personally from his power (cf. 6:53–56).

Surely it is appropriate for people to come to Jesus asking him to meet their needs in order that they may live a whole life. But if this is all they do they have misunderstood him. They have made him into a supernatural vending machine.

The Friends and Family (3:21, 31–35)

Many commentators think that (as Mark presents the incidents) Jesus' family "sent to him and called him" (3:31) for the same reason his friends "went out to seize him" (3:21); they thought he was " 'beside himself.' " (3:21) They misunderstood him to be a "crazy" religious fanatic. They interpreted his ability to cast out demons, heal the sick, liberate the captive as a form of *mental derangement.* And as he stood within the rising tide of emotion that was surging around him they feared for his safety and tried to take him home. Notice Jesus was not speaking in tongues, or talking about his personal religious experience, or coercing people into some particular profession of faith. He was simply helping people, meeting their immediate and desperate needs.

The Scribes (3:22–27)

The scribes (the professional theologians who *knew* what God had said and how he had acted—what he was *supposed* to say and how he was *supposed* to act) said, " 'He is possessed by Beelzebul, and by the prince of demons he casts out the demons.' " (3:22) Because they are threatened by his popularity, offended by his unorthodox ways, and blinded by their refusal to open their eyes to the possibility that God is speaking and acting directly in a new way through this Rabbi (cf. 1:21–28), they say he is representative of Satan. If we think of sonship as functional and define the son as the active agent, then, in a sense, they are calling him "the son of Satan." (Contrast this with 3:11.) The scribes misunderstand Jesus to be just the opposite from what he is! (For a suggestion of why they do this see the section titled "Conflict in Palestine," above.) The absurdity of this view is shown by Jesus through two parabolic sayings: "The Divided Kingdom" (3:24–26) and "The Plunder of the Strong Man's House" (3:27). The meanings of these analogies are obvious: (1) Jesus is casting out demons. Would an agent of Satan be routing his own troops? If so, a revolution has occurred in the diabolic realm and its self-destruction is certain. (2) Jesus is the man who has entered the strong man's house and is plundering his goods. In order to be doing this he must have bound the "strong man." The strong man is Satan.

Three questions: Do people today ever say of God's action, "That is the work of the devil"? If liberation and healing and wholeness of life are the results of governmental legislation, or civil demonstration, or social service can these be modes of God's action parallel to the evangelistic programs for the salvation of souls conducted through the church? If we no longer believe in demons and a personal devil (Satan), how can we translate the meaning of this passage into appropriate current concepts?

The Demons (3:11)

The "unclean spirits" (or demons) are the exception to the rule in Mark 3:7–35. They *understand* who Jesus is! "You are the Son of God." (3:11) What is Mark telling his original as well as his modern readers through this reference? Perhaps that those forces which oppose God are quicker and better able to recognize his Son speaking and acting for him in the world than are those who think they know precisely how God speaks and acts. At the very least Mark is insisting that God's word-deed in the world is to be defined by Jesus' word-deed in the Gospel. What then does Jesus' word-deed look like in this Gospel?

Note on the unforgivable sin: if one will read Mark 3:28–30 within its context (following 3:22–27), and verses 29–30 in parallel, the meaning of this troublesome text may be clarified. Blasphemy against the Holy Spirit (29) is equivalent to saying "He has an unclean spirit." (30) In other words it is calling the work of God the work of the devil, refusing to acknowledge the action of the Spirit and in fact attributing the movement of the Spirit to the force of evil. Insofar as one willfully persists in this attitude, this state of existence, it is impossible for God to break through with his forgiving and saving presence. He is refused entrance. He is kept outside. To refuse self-defensively to acknowledge the good as good, to call good evil is confounding! It is perverse. To continue to do this anesthetizes the religious and ethical sense, the faculty of truth-perception, the moral "existential self." It is, therefore, ultimately spiritually, morally, and personally *deadly*. "Light denied brings night." (Cf. Isa. 5:20.)

Teachings about the Kingdom
Mark 4:1-34

In the Synoptic Gospels (Matthew, Mark, and Luke, which can be "seen together" as having similar order, wording, and style), it appears that Jesus' typical method of teaching was the use of parables. The purpose of Jesus' parables was to clarify his message. Parables are short stories or brief sayings taken from common life and used as illustrations. They are comparisons or analogies (cf. 4:26-29, 30-32). (They are dynamic metaphors disclosing the extraordinary *in* the ordinary, the sacred *with* the secular, the gracious *through* the commonplace.) Ordinarily they make a single important point. They say that there is one telling way in which something is like something else. They engage the readers or hearers, asking them to participate in the situation, identify with the characters of the story, and allow the little drama to question them about to whom or what they are committed.

Occasionally several separate components of a parable (usually a story) correspond to different individual ideas or events which together make up the total meaning. This kind of parable lends itself to an allegorical interpretation. An example is the parable of "The Sower, the Seed, and the Soils." (4:2-9) The sower is Jesus (after him, his disciples, and in an ultimate sense, God). The seed is "the Word"—Jesus' announcement of the kingdom of God (later the disciples' proclamation of the gospel of salvation through Christ). The soils are the various types of persons who hear Jesus' word (subsequently the different kinds of lives which are confronted by the gospel).

An explanation of this parable is given in 4:14-20. Many modern commentators think that this interpretation originated in the early Christian community. Undoubtedly it would find immediate and relevant application in a conflict situation. Its meaning for us today is also obvious. We must simply translate its terms into our contemporary experiences. In so doing, however, let us not miss the major positive thrust: In spite of all the regrettable loss (4:14-19) the word *is* heard, accepted, and obeyed by many faithful persons. This fragile but fertile seed *does* live and grow and bear much fruit within receptive and productive soil. This is most remarkable. Perhaps we should retitle this brief illustrative anecdote "The Parable of the Abundant Harvest."

The other verbal analogies which Mark has collected in chapter 4 are short parabolic sayings.

Indiscriminate Preaching (4:21–23)

What should Jesus do if many will not listen to his word? What should disciples do if many will not respond to the gospel? Should Jesus withdraw his word from the multitude and save it for a faithful few? Should disciples hold back the gospel from the masses and preserve it for the religious remnant? No. You do not hide a light under a basket or a bed. You put it on a stand. From there the light shines out upon every object in the room. Jesus' word of the kingdom and the church's proclamation of the gospel are intended for all.

That reign of God, that authoritative presence of the Ruler, which in the past has been hidden (vs. 22), is now being disclosed in and through Jesus and must be offered to all (vss. 21–22; cf. Rom. 16:25f.; Eph. 3:9; 1 Cor. 2:7; Col. 1:26ff.). Is it possible to preach without also acting? Can the spoken word be separated from the demonstrated word? For Jesus it could not. " 'If any man has ears to hear, let him hear.' " (Vs. 23)

The Measure of Hearing Is Determined by the Measure of Giving (4:24)

The very nature of the Word which is heard is such that comprehension of it, real experience of its all encompassing significance, is determined by the degree to which it is transmitted to others. What a startling thought! How much people really understand the gospel of forgiveness and obedience, of freedom and responsibility equals how much they have communicated it to others! How can this be? Perhaps an illustration will help clarify the meaning here: a teacher learns as much, and more, in the act of teaching as she or he does in study and preparation.

A Fact of Kingdom Life (4:25)

If, for example, a person is studying math, he or she must learn lessons one through four well in order to learn lesson five. " 'To him who has will more be given.' " If a person does not know well lessons one through four, lesson five will make no sense, and whatever one may have understood in the previous lessons will soon prove useless. " 'From him who has not, even what he has will be taken away.' " This is the way it is with hearing the Word. This is also a fact of life in the kingdom. The more one is obedient, the more one perceives and receives. The less one is obedient, the less one perceives and receives. And even that little original meaningfulness will vanish!

The Power Is God's and the Time Is Now (4:26–29)

This parable is found only in Mark. What is the main idea which Jesus is communicating through it? Interpreters answer this question in various ways. Perhaps the central message is two-fold. (1) The kingdom is the result of God's work, the product of God's power—*not a human* product. " 'The seed ... sprout and grow, he knows not how. The earth produces of itself...' " The necessity of sowing is not denied. But human cultivation is not even mentioned. The emphasis is obviously upon the divine "miracle" of life, growth, and yield. Humankind does not "build" or "bring in" the kingdom of God. God himself establishes his reign. The harvest is in his hands. This is a strong word of encouragement to all sowers of the seed, in any age and in any place. This is also a faithful reminder of the ultimacy and supremacy of God's being, of the creative and sustaining power of God, and the ultimate dependence of persons upon God. (2) The time is now. "The kingdom is at hand." The preliminaries are over. The main event is beginning. Moses, the prophets, John the Baptist have come and gone. *This is the moment of God's action and the person's decision.* Both center in the One who speaks these words: " 'first the blade, then the ear, then the full grain in the ear. But when the grain is ripe, at once he puts in the sickle, because *the harvest has come.*' " (Author's emphasis; cf. Joel 3:13.) To those who accept the meaning of Mark this announcement is perpetually present. This instant and the next, and the next, they are called to acknowledge the authority of God, accept his grace and obey his command.

The Hiddenness of the Kingdom (4:30–34)

A mustard seed is so tiny, so fragile, so insignificant. Just by looking at it who would suspect that it has within it a large shrub? No one. The kingdom of God is like that. It too is hidden, even in the present. Outward appearances and external circumstances would deny its reality. World history and current events would repudiate its existence. But it is there. In a sense the seed and the shrub are the same. "For God's kingdom comes in concealment, indeed even in spite of failure."[20] People of faith know this. Eyes of faith see this. Because they have looked at the *crucified Jesus* and have seen *the living Lord.* What an astounding, supportive, and sustaining word for disciples caught in conflict in powerful pagan Rome of the first century or secular self-sufficient America in the twentieth! What a claiming, commanding, and challenging word to the church in any era—to fear not its anonymity, its participation, its involvement within the world.

The Mighty Power Of Jesus
Mark 4:35—6:6

This section of Mark's Gospel contains five significant "forms"—four "miracle stories" and one "pronouncement story": "The Stilling of the Storm" (4:35–41); "The Gerasene Demoniac" (5:1–20); "The Woman with the Continuing Hemorrhage" (5:25–34); "The Raising of Jairus' Daughter" (5:21–24, 35–43); "The Prophet Without Honor" (6:1–6). For a brief discussion of the use of forms in the composition of the Gospels see the section on "Form Criticism" above.

The Stilling of the Storm (4:35–41)

This story, of course, could be understood merely on the level of the miraculous. Several physical details might suggest original eye-witness remembrance. It is evening; the disciples take Jesus with them, just as he is; "other boats" also leave the shore; he is "in the stern, asleep on the cushion"; the vessel is about to be swamped and the disciples are terrified, afraid that they are about to be drowned. Whether we approach this story as an objective, historical account, or as a dramatic teaching shaped by the early church, or both, through it three basic ideas are disclosed. (1) The disciples lack faith (vss. 38 and 40). Although they have been with Jesus some time and have watched him healing people and casting out demons, they still are not able to trust their own lives to him. Their question is a sharp cry of fearful indignation: "Teacher! Don't you even care if we die?" (2) The disciples do know their only possible source of help in their moment of crisis. When their very existence is threatened they turn directly to Jesus (vs. 38). (3) The power of Jesus is of divine origin and therefore sufficient. Only God himself can command and control the forces of his creation (vss. 39, 41).

There is, however, another level of meaning at which this story must be understood, another context of history—other than the original situation of Jesus and the disciples—in which it must be comprehended. This is the contextual level of the young church, and by conceptual extension the older community of the faithful today.

Undoubtedly, by the time Mark included this story in his Gospel, it had circulated widely and gained symbolic significance. Early in its history the church was represented by the figure of a boat. The stormy sea for prescience persons, for the mythic mentality of the ancient world, was the reflection of primordial chaos (cf. Gen. 1:1–2) or the death-dealing instrument of the Evil One. It continually threatened the existence of order and life. For Christians in the Roman Empire it symbolized the hostile environment into which they found themselves thrust, the ostensible realm of Satan in which they lived and died. This story should be read not only as a report but also as a parable.

Not just once, but often, the ship of the church found itself caught in a ferocious storm. (Remember the Neronian persecution of 63 and the Jewish Revolt of 66–70 A.D.) Individual disciples, because they were "in the same boat" with the One who was crucified, often found themselves in the midst of a tempest, in the throes of suffering, in the clutches of death (cf. 2 Cor. 11:23–28). In both fearful anguish and faithful abandonment they cried out: " 'Do you not care if we perish?' " (" 'My God, my God, why hast thou forsaken me?' " Mark 15:33) It was crucial for them to know when the sea was rough and the waves beat upon them—and particularly when the ship was actually wrecked—that the One who was with them was the One who "rebuked the wind, and said to the sea, 'Peace! Be still!' " (Cf. Pss. 65:7; 107:23–32.) It was he who was in control, not the forces of destruction, regardless of what happened. It was only because they lacked faith that they thought otherwise. And so may it be today for modern disciples. Therefore, they may also hear, "Why are you afraid? Have you no faith?"

But let us not for a moment forget that it was only as *they had ventured out into the sea with him in the boat and were caught with him in the storm* that their lack of faith was matched by his power and they were able to ask, " 'Who then is this, that even wind and sea obey him?' " They were not standing safe and secure on the shore watching the scene on the sea.

The Gerasene Demoniac (5:1–20)

This story may be interpreted as a counterpart to "The Stilling of the Storm." The sea is symbolic for the realm of the demonic—the possessive, destructive, death-dealing forces in the world, in ordinary existence. The swine rush headlong over the cliff and are drowned in the sea. The unclean spirits are driven back to their original abode, and there they perish. The Divine defeats the demonic. Thus the power of Jesus is shown to be the power of God himself, and the effective results of his power are manifest in freedom, wholeness, and life.

The Woman with the Continuing Hemorrhage (5:25–34)

Here again a person is in the extremity of need. The woman is physically ill and religiously isolated. (According to Jewish law she is unclean.) She is practically dead. She has been this way for twelve years and apparently there is no hope for improvement (vss. 25f.). Unlike the disciples she is not a close associate of Jesus; she is just one of the crowd. Unlike the disciples in the boat she has faith (vs. 28). Could it be that Mark is reminding some of his readers that there are people "out there" who do not claim to know Jesus like the disciples do, but who have more faith in him than they do, and that these faithful touch his garment and are healed through means which would probably be unacceptable to them? The result of the woman's faith and Jesus' power is health and life. The operation of Jesus' power is dependent upon the woman's faith (vss. 28f., 34). How would you translate the meanings of this story into terms of contemporary human existence?

The Raising of Jairus' Daughter (5:21–24, 35–43)

This story reiterates that "the Son of God" who announces "the kingdom" demonstrates its character as life-affirming and life-preserving. The power of God which Jesus employs must ordinarily be met by faith in order to be effective. Even potential enemies (Jairus is a ruler of the synagogue) who come to Jesus in trust are not turned away.

The Prophet Without Honor (6:1–6)

Perhaps the most striking and penetrating words in this story are these: " 'Where did this man get all this? What is the wisdom given to him? What mighty works are wrought by his hands! Is not this the carpenter, the son of Mary and brother of James and Joses and Judas and Simon, and are not his sisters here with us?' And they took offense at him." (6:2f.) At least a part of Mark's meaning might be expressed today, for believers and non-believers alike, in words such as these: Jesus is just too ordinary, too human, to be special. We cannot have that! We will not allow it. But that is precisely the point. The extraordinary comes in, with, and through the ordinary! The "Son of God" comes as one of us within the midst of our common, human, interpersonal life. This means *our* common life is his. Our family, vocational, sexual, social—all our life is both redeemed and claimed by God. This is what we cannot take. *He is too common and therefore too relevant!* Because of this we reject him. And in such a situation he can "do no mighty work," except place his hands upon a few sick people and heal them. It is among *his own* that he is astonished by unbelief.

Disciples Called and Commissioned
Mark 6:7–56

The background reading in Mark's Gospel for the following brief interpretive reflections includes the following: "The Call and Commission of the Disciples" (6:7–13); "The Death of John the Baptist" (6:14–29); "The Feeding of the Five Thousand" (6:30–44); "Jesus Walking on the Water" (6:45–52); "The Landing at Gennesaret" (6:53–56).

The Call and Commission of the Disciples (6:7–13)

Mark 3:13–15 should be read in connection with the paragraph before us. There the vocation of the disciples is described. They are called and commissioned: (1) "to be with him" (3:14); (2) "to be sent out to preach" (3:14); and (3) "to have authority to cast out demons." (3:15) In short, in fellowship with him and in obedience to him, they are to do the very same things he does. They are to carry forward his ministry. They are to proclaim the word of judgment and grace. They are to set people free and promote wholeness of life (demon possession means bondage and brokenness).

How are modern disciples fulfilling this call and carrying out this commission? Are they "with him" wherever he is? Where *is* he? How do they get "with him"? How are they preaching what he proclaimed? " 'The kingdom of God is at hand. Repent and believe in the gospel.' " (Cf. 6:12.) Should it sound something like this? The reign of sin and death is ended. Forgiveness and life are offered to all who will receive them. Therefore, leave that old mode of being. Enter the new. Trust that this proclamation is true and act upon it. The "principalities and powers," the forces that enslave and the structures that kill are not the determinative factors in human existence. They are *not* the rulers of this world. The liberating life-giving God is the absolute and active authority (although the old regime still violently resists his government). Therefore, turn from fearful obeisance to those non-deities, from sinful acceptance of their deceitful claims to save through material wealth, social prestige, and self-security. They are not in control. Therefore, do not let yourselves be controlled by them. Believe this astounding good news: "in Christ Jesus you are all sons of God, through faith." (Gal. 3:26) And if sons, then heirs. Adult masters over the estate. Vice-regents under the king. You have been given "dominion" over all the "creatures" for the welfare of humanity (Gen. 1:26; Ps. 8). Therefore, do not let them use you. Use them responsibly for the glory of God and the benefit of people.

It is one thing simply to say these things; it is another thing to communicate them convincingly. Therefore, "He charged them to take nothing for their journey except a staff; no bread, no bag, no money in their belts; but to wear sandals and not put on two tunics." (6:8f.) If contemporary disciples cannot take this command literally how can they best manifest *the urgency of the mission and the dependence of the missioners* which it expresses?

The very light traveling equipment which the disciples are told to take (6:8f.) means not only that they go out urgently and dependently, but also that they go out in haste (cf. also 6:10f.). They are not to be slowed down with cumbersome baggage. They must not tarry, for the time is short." 'The kingdom of God *is at hand*!' " (Author's emphasis.) *Now* is the moment of decision, commitment, obedience. The original New Testament church (the Twelve) went out into the world streamlined, stripped for action.

According to 6:7, Jesus sent his disciples out "two by two." Why was this? "Because in Jewish custom every promise needed two witnesses (Deut. 17:6), and these messengers were to give testimony not only to the word of God but also to the response of the towns."[21] This means two things: (1) The messengers were held responsible for proclaiming the word in truth and with clarity. (2) The hearers were held responsible for responding to the word—either positively or negatively.

Portraits of Saving Personhood (6:14–56)

In Mark's account of the death of John the Baptist (6:14–29) the reader is given a preview of what awaits Jesus and his faithful disciples. In the story of the feeding of the five thousand (6:35–44) we see the Messiah, the Shepherd-King, feeding his flock (cf. Isa. 40:10f.) and teaching his undershepherds what the real food of life is—*himself* (cf. John 6:27, 28, 35). This is by no means all that is in this many splendored story. But this affirmation—that Jesus is sustenance and the source of strength for those who follow him—is reiterated in the story of Jesus walking on the water (6:45–52). The boat (the church) is not making much headway against the wind and rough sea (the hostile world). Jesus comes to the disciples, but they cannot believe it is he. He speaks to them: " 'Take heart, it is I; have no fear.' " (Cf. Exod. 3:14.) "The loaves" (vs. 52) signify that he who calls and commissions and sends the disciples (preachers, exorcisers, healers, undershepherds) out into the world goes with them to supply their deepest need (cf. 6:35–44). This was "gospel" for the church in Rome. It may yet be good news for the church in contemporary culture. According to Mark's portrayal, the closest associates of Jesus found it difficult to understand and believe (6:52).

When Religion Is Vital It Is Not Exclusive
Mark 7:1—8:26

In this interpretive reflection let us center our attention upon the passage in 7:1–15 and the topic derived from it. Only brief references will be made to the remainder of this section of Mark's Gospel (7:16–8:26). These will attempt to demonstrate the conceptual relation of the several units of material found here; or, to put it another way, to answer the question, "Why did Mark select these particular sayings and stories from those available to him and group them together in this place?" The following outline of Mark 7:1–8:26 will suggest a preliminary answer. It is obviously interpretive: "Real Religion, Not Hollow Ritual" (7:1–8); "Responsible Obedience, Not Rigid Legalism" (7:9–13); "Internal Attitude Determines External Action" (7:14–23); "The Kingdom Is for All" (7:24–8:10); "No Sign for Those Who Are Unreceptive" (8:11–13); "The Leaven of Disbelief or the Bread of Faith" (8:14–21); "Believing Is Seeing." (8:22–26)

Evidence which strongly suggests that Mark's Gospel (in its final edition) is written primarily for non-Jewish Christians (or congregations which include Gentiles) within the Roman Empire (outside of Palestine) is made obvious in the passages before us in several ways. In 7:3f. he feels it necessary to explain certain Jewish practices of ceremonial washing. He inserts an interpretation in 7:19*b*, which his Gentle readers would welcome greatly and which would have direct bearing upon the Jewish-Gentile conflict within the church in Rome (and by clear implication upon any schism within the church at any place and at any time caused by one group's insistence upon adherence to a code which predetermines that certain things are generically "clean" and others "unclean"). He uses stories about Jesus going outside "The House of Israel" and there exorcising demons (7:24–30) and healing (7:31–37) in response to Gentile faith. It is even probable that Mark intends "The Feeding of the Four Thousand" (8:1–10) to be understood as having occurred among the Gentiles (a supplementary parallel to "The Feeding of the Five Thousand" (6:30–44) which took place among the Jews).

The one affirmation that unifies the separate sayings and stories of 7:1–8:26 is that Jesus, the gospel, and the kingdom are *not confined* to any particular ethnic or cultural group but are *open to all believers*. Barriers of tradition (7:1–23) and race (7:24–8:10) are broken down by Christ. They do not exist within the community of faith when religion is vital.

Before reading the comments on the individual passages which follow it would be appropriate to review the relevant sections above under the headings "Conflict in Palestine" (especially the part which discusses Jesus' attitude of *freedom from death-dealing legalism to life-giving love*) and "Conflict in the Roman World" (particularly the brief description of the cleavage between *Gentile Christian and Jewish Christian*).

Real Religion, Not Hollow Ritual (7:1–8)

One fundamental and all-encompassing "commandment of God" was: "'You shall be holy; for I the LORD your God am holy.'" (Lev. 19:2) In an honest and sincere attempt to defend, define, and apply to life such basic laws as this (cf. Lev. 22:1–16), serious and pious interpreters had produced numerous rules and regulations commonly called "the tradition of the elders." (7:3, 5, 8, 9, 13) Apparently by the first century A.D. this "tradition" included a ritual washing of the hands before meals. Strict Jews or Jewish Christians who still followed this tradition would be defiled by handling money and goods in the pagan Roman market place (7:4). The Pharisees and scribes are so concerned with these formal and ceremonial practices that they have forgotten the original commandment (7:8). Indeed, by their total absorption in the external ritual they have neglected and negated the inner intent of the law—a consecrated response of the whole self to the being of God through all the relations of human existence. Furthermore, we must ask, are these people using the mechanical function of "the tradition" as a substitute for real religion, as a shield against the radical call to commitment, full-hearted worship, and single-minded obedience? The questions which this word of Jesus might address to individual disciples today are numerous. They may also be hard to hear.

Responsible Obedience, Not Rigid Legalism (7:9–13)

This saying of Jesus illustrates how people reject the commandment of

God in order to keep their tradition (7:8f.). Support and care of parents in their old age was expected of children as one expression of their obedience to God through the fifth commandment (7:10; Exod. 20:12). But according to the scribal legislation (the currently accepted practice), "if a son had made a vow to offer to God, or to the Temple, property which was later needed to support his parents, he should give to this vow priority over his family obligation."[22] It is probable that in many cases the money was simply dedicated verbally (or pledged) but actually retained for personal use. In other words, one simply employed the tradition as an excuse for doing what one wanted to do rather than what one ought to do. This meant that a secondary and highly questionable human code took precedence over the fundamental law of God. Rigid legalism often replaced responsible obedience. And this Jesus condemned.

Internal Attitude Determines External Action (7:14–23)

Jesus' parable is really quite self-explanatory. One wonders why the disciples did not understand it. (This is, probably, another illustration of Mark's theme of the "obtuseness of the disciples.") What people *do*, the kinds of things they *do*, are determined by their inner thoughts, desires, motives. Therefore, it is not external objects which they use, food or drink which they take into themselves that make them "unclean." Nothing in God's creation is evil, or sinful in itself (7:19b; cf. Rom. 14). It is those internal attitudes which result in sinful and destructive acts (7:20–23) *or* faithful and loving deeds which are definitive and determinitive. "As a man thinketh in his heart so is he." Awareness of this fact should save Mark's readers and hearers from inhibiting and crippling petty legalism. It should also cause them to ask themselves seriously, "Who am I inside?" It should remind them that while they must continue to work to realize love and justice through all the structures of society, a permeating and permanent change must ultimately come through a change of human hearts. It should also correct the sentimental subjectivism which suggests that it doesn't matter what I *do*, if anything, all that counts is what I feel in my heart. Neither the objective action nor the subjective feeling is alone valid. Both are necessary, and a congruity between the two is essential for vital religion and authentic life.

The Christ Must Suffer—His Disciples Must Follow
Mark 8:27–37

This brief passage (8:27–37) is packed with meaning. For the purpose of our brief study here it may be divided into three parts: "You Are the Christ" (vss. 27–30); "The Son of Man Must Suffer" (vss. 31–33); "Losing Life and Saving It" (vss. 34–37). As we come to interpret this account of Peter's confession and Jesus' sayings about suffering it is important that we remember that Mark's Gospel was written after the crucifixion and the resurrection. The original events and the actual words of Jesus have been recalled within, shaped by, and applied to the contemporary situation of the church, the community of believers.

You Are the Christ (8:27–30)

Jesus and his disciples are in the road. (It was common practice for teachers to instruct their students as they walked along together, the master in the lead. Followers in Rome, and elsewhere, knew this "road" well.) They are "on the way," going to Jerusalem, where he must confront the opposition with his proclamation and his person. (Recall that for Mark, and his readers, Jerusalem is symbolic of more than merely a geographical location.) It is necessary to enter the royal city of God to have the fundamental issue clearly drawn, the basic question sharply framed. Who is right? Let the King decide! It is inevitable that he meet the official representatives of the orthodox religion on their home ground, within their stronghold, to present them with the choice, to force them to take a stand, for him or against him. He (and the reader) knows what the result will be (vs. 31). In the meantime his disciples must be taught who he is and the way he is to go. And they too must decide (again): yes or no. Conscious of the current verdict of others (vs. 28) they must make their own profession. The general populace thinks he is significant. They say he is John the Baptist resurrected, or Elijah—that is, the forerunner and preparer for the new age. Or he is a prophet come to announce God's action in the present. Both alternatives are high estimates. Both stop one step short. "Who do *you* say that I am?" As the spokesman for the group, Peter replies: " 'You are the Christ.' " (Vs. 29) You are the Messiah, the Anointed one, the designated agent of God, the deliverer of Israel.

Is this not the right answer? Why then does Jesus, as Mark portrays him, immediately charge them "to tell no one about him"? (Vs. 30) Some scholars say that here we have another illustration of *Mark's* explanation of why Jesus was not recognized as the Christ before his death (cf.1:43f.; 3:12; 5:43). (See above on "The Messianic Secret.") Others see here a more historical reflection. It is *good* that Jesus' disciples have come to the conclusion that he is the Messiah and this he gladly accepts. But he knows they do not yet understand the kind of Messiah he must be. Undoubtedly they have decided that he is the One in whom the hope of Israel is to be fulfilled. Perhaps they could be no more specific than that. But if they go out now proclaiming Jesus as the Messiah many will take him for a military conqueror and a political leader. He certainly is not that and he does not want that false report to get around. Therefore he commands silence while he *reinterprets* for them the nature of Messiahship, while he instructs them in the way that he must go (and by implication the way that those who follow him must also go).

The Son of Man Must Suffer (8:31–33)

He begins "to teach them that the Son of man must suffer... and be killed." (Vs. 31) This is the method by which he will deliver and redeem. But this is a strange word to their ears. A suffering and dying Messiah? Who ever heard of such? Nonsense! Victory in rejection and death? Impossible! Therefore, Peter takes him and begins to rebuke him. The Greek words suggest that Peter may have drawn him close, or even put his arm around Jesus' shoulders in a gesture of patronizing protection as he attempted to admonish and correct him. But Peter is out of place. The position of a disciple is *behind* his master (vs. 33f.). Where he stands and as he speaks now, Peter is nothing less than the personification of Satan! He is tempting Jesus, just as Satan did before in the wilderness, to try it some other way. For men "nothing succeeds like success." And the right route to success is through popularity, prestige, and power. This is not God's way (vs. 33). He goes through the cross. Thus Mark presents Jesus.

Losing Life and Saving It (8:34–37)

The invitation is extended again and to all (vs. 34). The original call to discipleship is reissued. "Now that I have begun to explain to you what it involves, do you still want to stay with it? The choice is yours. Will anyone else come?" Discipleship, *following after Jesus* (he is out front moving on) means going the very same way he goes (vss. 31, 34). It means disowning one's self, giving one's self to him, placing one's self at his disposal, allowing him to determine who one is and what one does. It means accepting "the last consequences of obedience"—the cross, taking the final risk of identification with Jesus—death.[23] It means continued allegiance regardless of what one must face along the way.

But paradoxically and amazingly, it also means *life, the realization of true selfhood.* For people who would save their lives (physical existence or total self-security) will lose their real selves. People who attempt to define themselves apart from Christ, people who clutch protectively their own beings to themselves will kill them. But people who lose their lives as disciples, in the active service of Christ and the message of freedom and life in him, will realize true selfhood. For what have you actually got even if you gain the whole world and have given up your real selfhood for it?

For the disciples in the Roman Empire this was a daily decision. For them the choice was often phsycial existence and living death or physical death and real life. Seldom do disciples today in the Christian Western world have to make the decision in that form. But the choice is nevertheless daily, moment by moment, before them. And they make it—one way or another. For the disciple, "to live is Christ, and to die is gain." (Phil. 1:21)

Poverty and Riches: The Meaning of Discipleship
Mark 10

Chapter 10 in Mark's Gospel teaches (cf. 10:1) that participation in the kingdom of God (10:14f., 23f.), which is here identified with "eternal life" (10:17, 30) and "salvation" (10:26) is not the result of strict obedience to law (10:2–12, 17–22) but is rather God's gift (10:15, 27) to those who will receive it in childlike dependence (10:13–16) and humble trust (10:21f., 31, 42–45) expressed in discipleship (10:21, 28, 32–34). Through the story of "Blind Bartimaeus" (10:46–52), Mark illustrates the appropriate attitude and action of a follower of Jesus: awareness of "poverty" and "blindness"; desire to be healed; faith in the power of Jesus to "heal"; willingness to come after Jesus "on the way" to the cross. This man who receives his sight is contrasted with the self-sufficient "Rich Young Man" (10:17–22) and the personally ambitious "Sons of Zebedee" (10:35–45). The question which Mark is asking his readers is this: "can *you* see?"

To Lack One Thing Is to Lose All (10:17–22)

This well-known and oft-quoted story is also one of the most revealing in the Gospels (cf. Matt. 19:16–30; Luke 18:18–30). In verse 17 the writer purposefully notes that Jesus is again "setting out on his journey." He is on that "road" which leads finally to Jerusalem and what awaits him there (cf. vss. 32–34). A fine respectable young man runs up to Jesus, kneels before him, and asks him: " 'Good Teacher, what must I do to inherit eternal life?' " The urgency of this man is not to be doubted. His respect for Jesus is not to be denied. His sincerity is not to be questioned. He is quite serious. Furthermore, he is as good as any man (cf. vs. 18) and better than most. According to the law of God he claims to be blameless (cf. Phil. 3:6). " 'All these [things] I have observed from my youth.' " (Vs. 20) His statement may be impulsive but Jesus does not reject it. Rather, "looking upon him" Jesus loves him, wills his well-being. Therefore Jesus must tell him: " 'You lack one thing; go, sell what you have, and give to the poor, and you will have treasure in heaven; and come, follow me.' " (Vs. 21)

The one thing he lacks is not really something "more." Not more merit and credit, not more "possessions." In fact he possesses too much already—too much in which he trusts, on which he depends for his life. He has "great possessions," both material and moral. His problem is that he seeks to secure himself with these and thereby he prohibits himself the possibility of faith. The one thing he lacks is the willingness and ability to become a child again

(10:15)–defenseless, vulnerable, receptive, and utterly dependent upon the Father. He, therefore, not only must sell his property, but must also give the money which he makes on the transaction to those who are in poverty. For he must himself become "poor" in order to possess the greatest "wealth." And he must follow Jesus. The decision and the action are one. The crucial truth of this story must be sharply focused and clearly comprehended: "eternal life" and discipleship mean giving up any claim to self-sufficiency, any attempt to secure or save oneself—particularly through material prosperity and moral self-righteousness—and trusting Christ alone for life in the present as well as in "the age to come." (Vs. 30) In the first-century A.D. (as in the 20th) material prosperity and moral righteousness were often too simply equated!

Earthly Riches and Kingdom Wealth (10:23–31)

The thought of the preceding passage is carred forward into this series of sayings. The fact that it is simply impossible for a man who trusts in his material wealth and depends upon it for his total existence to participate in the kingdom of God is reiterated by Jesus. The "rich man" of verses 23–25 is (representatively) the same man who "went away sorrowful." (Vs. 22) Jesus uses a proverbial saying to declare how completely irreconcilable are dependence upon material security and faithful discipleship (vs. 25). He is not saying that all wealthy people are automatically excluded from salvation (cf. vs. 26). He *is* recognizing and emphasizing the fact, however, that financial affluence may be a serious obstacle in the path of one who wants to follow him. It is so easy to *trust* in riches. But it is not impossible even for a wealthy man to be saved! " 'With men it is impossible, but not with God; for all things are possible with God.' " (Vs. 27) What is this "impossible" thing which Jesus says *is* "possible" with God? *Not* that a rich man can follow Jesus without becoming "poor," but that a rich man *can* become "poor," can become a child (10:15).[24] Even a rich man can become "poor in spirit." (Matt. 5:3) By the grace of God even a man who has many material possessions can realize his abject poverty, his state of absolute insecurity, and the necessity of his total dependence upon God for life (cf. Rom. 1:16–17; 3:9–8:39; Phil. 3:1–16).

It may be that Peter understands what Jesus is saying and in his statement (vs. 28) implicitly acknowledges that it is God who has enabled the disciples to get "on the way" with Jesus.[25] Or we may have here the beginning of a new and separate short section in this chapter.[26] In either case the meaning of Jesus' reply in verses 29–31 is clear. Disciples do not only give up, they also gain. They may leave behind "everything" but they also receive "everything" and more (vs. 30). The rich young man possesses everything but lacks one thing. And because he lacks this one thing he really possesses nothing. The disciples lack everything. But because they lack everything they possess one thing—the kingdom of God or "eternal life" or "true selfhood" or "authentic existence." Even in this present time they receive abundantly. They have left their blood relatives and their real estates in order to follow Jesus and proclaim the gospel. But they have gotten a new family and a new home (the church)—"with persecutions." (Vs. 30) The Christians in Rome understood these words well. As the church in America corporately, and its members as individual Christians, leave the security of "lands" and "houses" and follow Christ out into the world today they may also know their meaning. But let them remember: " 'many that are first will be last, and the last first.' " (Vs. 31) Or, as we read it in 8:35: " 'For whoever would save his life will lose it; and whoever loses his life for my sake and the gospel's will save it.' "

The Authority of Jesus
Mark 11—12

Several passages in chapters 11 and 12 may be understood as reminders by Mark for Christians and declarations to all others of the authority of Jesus: "The Entry into Jerusalem" (11:1–10), "The Cleansing of the Temple" (11:15–19), "The Debate with the Jewish Leaders" (11:27–33), "The Parable of the Son and the Tenants" (12:1–11), and "The Question about Taxes to Caesar" (12:13–17). The interpretations offered here will focus upon "The Debate with the Jewish Leaders" and "The Question about Taxes to Caesar." Both of these incidents appear in Mark in the form of "controversy stories," and the primary concern of each is to communicate an important "pronouncement" of Jesus (11:29–33, esp. vs. 33, and 12:17). For a brief discussion of pronouncement stories using 12:13–17 as an illustration see the section on "Form Criticism." After considering these two stories we will listen briefly to "The Great Commandment" (12:28–34). The section in the thematic essay *"Christ and Conflict"* particularly relevant to these interpretive reflections is the one titled "Conflict in Palestine."

The Debate with the Jewish Leaders (11:27–33)

The "chief priests and the scribes and the elders" find Jesus walking in the Temple (the abode of God and the seat of divine rule) and put the question to him directly: " 'By what authority are you doing these things, or who gave you this authority to do them?' " (11:28)

Some commentators think that the phrase "these things" refers to Jesus' cleansing of the Temple. Others say that it is the teaching of Jesus that is meant. Others believe that it is Jesus' whole ministry of preaching, teaching, and acting (including healing, etc.) which is signified. This last view is perhaps the most likely.

Rather than answering directly the question of the religious leaders, Jesus asks them a question in turn. This was "a method common in

Rabbinical discussion."[27] Jesus is not, therefore, really evading the issue. For if they had been able to say that the baptism of John was "from heaven" (that is, that the whole work of John, including his role as the forerunner, had been the will of God) then they would have been admitting that John was right, that Jesus was in fact the Messiah, and that his authority was from God himself. Jesus' own approval of John (cf. 1:9; Matt. 11:2–19; Luke 7:18–35) makes this claim in Mark implicit, as does the argument of the leaders among themselves in verse 31.

In this story, concluding with Jesus' refusal to answer the question directly (vs. 33), Mark is pronouncing and proclaiming a redefinition of Messiahship (through the cross) and the quality of divine authority (Jesus' life, death, and resurrection); also Mark is saying that it is necessary for people to decide about Jesus for themselves *in faith.* Although the answer is available in Jesus' counter-question about John and in the parable of "The Son and the Tenants" which follows (12:1–11), at this point the reader or hearer is left with the question: "By what authority *does* Jesus do 'These things'? In other words, who *is* he?" What do *you* say?

The church in every place and age has answered that he does "these things" by the authority of God and that he, therefore, is the Lord over *all of life*. This means, of course, that the church is to allow him to define its worship and its work, that individual Christians are to allow him to define their vocations and their recreations. It means that as he enters "the Temple" (the church) today and announces, " 'My house shall be called a house of prayer for all the nations,' " the congregation should listen to him and act accordingly. Any authority claimed in the name of Jesus and employed by Christians within either "the church" or "the world," is to be characterized by the means and the ends of his authority. As Mark portrays Jesus he is most typically *authoritative,* crowned with thorns, and enthroned on a cross (15:16–39; cf. Phil. 2:5–11).

The Question about Taxes to Caesar (12:13–17)

The attempt is made to trick Jesus into either being a traitor to Israel by acknowledging that the Jews should pay the hated poll tax to Rome with coins on which the idolatrous name and image of Tiberius Caesar were printed, or being a traitor to Rome by declaring that the Jews should rebelliously withhold this tribute. The first alternative is tantamount to rejecting the authority of God. The second is equivalent to rejecting the authority of the state. " 'Is it lawful to pay taxes to Caesar, or not?' " If Jesus simply answers yes, he will imply disloyalty to God and he will repel the people. If he simply answers no, he will deny allegiance to the emperor and he will surely invite death for treason. Jesus does neither. He calls for a coin from his questioners and thereby puts them on the defensive. What are they doing with that coin anyway? Does not the fact that they possess on their persons this money with the image of Tiberius engraved on it question *their* unequivocal loyalty to God? But does not the image also prove that "this money was coined by the emperor and therefore belonged to him"?[28] They are caught in their own trap and the answer to their question is a decision which they must make.

To suggest a contemporary translation: this question may be as relevant today as it was in the first century A.D. What must I render to the state and what must I render to God? Much of the time there is no fundamental conflict. But neither can "God and country" simply be equated. (Unfortunately this is often done, particularly in time of war.) *For the Christian there is no loyalty higher than that which he or she bears to God alone.* When a person's honest commitment to God conflicts with civil law or national policy he or she has no choice but to obey God rather than human authorities and take the consequences (Acts 5:29).

The Great Commandment (12:28–34)

Jesus is put on the spot. He is asked in effect, "If you had to sum up the totality of our religion, what would you say?" He replies: "Active allegiance of the whole self to God above all else, and the same kind and degree of active concern for the total well-being of our fellow human beings as we have right now for ourselves." (Cf. Deut. 6:4 and Lev. 19:18.) How this two-fold commandment may be expressed in human lives could provide discussion for another entire book, and more! But perhaps this is precisely the problem: this commandment has been discussed too much and obeyed too little. Probably most people already know what it *means*. It only remains for us to *enact it* in personal relationships, in families, in society as a whole.

A Symbolic Supper and a Time of Testing
Mark 14:22–26, 32–42

Comments on the place of chapter 13 within Mark's overall literary structure and theological purpose have been made in several places within the thematic essays above. All of the material in Mark's "Passion Narrative" (14:1–16:8) is interrelated and highly colored by its origin, preservation, and use within the early church. It served as a literary vehicle for interpreting the significance of Jesus' death, for exhorting the community to steadfast loyalty to Christ in the face of persecution, for ordering the services of worship, especially the celebration of the eucharist. Let us reflect briefly upon two scenes of this evangelical and liturgical drama.

The Last Supper (14:22–26)

As Mark presents it, "The Last Supper" was originally a celebration of The Feast of Passover by Jesus and his disciples (14:12–14). There are a number of reasons, evidenced in chapters 14–16 in Mark, why the identification of The Last Supper with the Passover Feast is historically problematic.[29] However, we must remember that Mark is not primarily interested in the details of factual history. He is proclaiming the *significance* of Jesus' life, death, and resurrection. Also he is employing traditional material which has been shaped by its function in the life of the believing community. By the time Mark wrote his Gospel, even as is the custom today, the narrative of the Last Supper was used in the liturgy of the Sacrament. We shall, therefore, interpret this passage within its Markan context and as an expression of the faith of the worshiping church.

"The Blessing (vs. 22) . . . is an act of thanksgiving to God, and, according to Jewish usage, would take the form: 'Praised be Thou, O Lord our God, King of the Universe, who bringest forth bread from the earth,' or, . . . 'Blessed art Thou, our Father in heaven, who givest us to-day the bread necessary for us'."[30]

The Passover Feast recalled and made contemporary for the participating Jewish family the event of the Exodus (Exod. 11–14). It, therefore, symbolized the gracious action of God which resulted in the deliverance of the people from captivity. It meant freedom *from* bondage and death, *to* liberty and life. In an all-encompassing sense this is precisely what "The Christ Event" meant for the early Christians in Mark's community and elsewhere throughout the Roman World. From the first century to the present time the church has proclaimed this meaning in its message and celebrated this meaning in the sacrament of "The Lord's Supper."

Within the setting of the Passover celebration the reference to the "blood of the covenant which is poured out for many" may point to the sacrifice of the paschal lamb and the sign " 'on the lintel and on the two doorposts' " (Exod. 12:23) which protected the Hebrews during the night of death. This same function is performed in a fashion beyond the merely physical by Jesus on the cross for all who will believe.

Or "the blood of the covenant" may signify that in and through the life and death of Jesus a "new" covenant is offered to all who will participate in it. The Old Testament allusions in this case would be Exodus 24:8 and Jeremiah 31:31–34. At Sinai this sprinkling of the blood of the covenant symbolized the binding of God and the people together through the law. The *purpose* of the law was the *life* of the people (cf. Exod. 19:3–6). The "new" covenant Jesus seals with his blood (his life) fulfills the "old" completely and extends it to all who will *follow him.* Where does he lead and how does he go there? To the cross in obedient love (14:32–41). According to the prophet Jeremiah:

> "Behold, the days are coming, says the LORD, when I will make a new covenant with the house of Israel and the house of Judah, not like

the covenant which I made with their fathers when I took them by the hand to bring them out of the land of Egypt, my covenant which they broke, though I was their husband, says the LORD. But this is the covenant which I will make with the house of Israel after those days, says the LORD: I will put my law within them, and I will write it upon their hearts; and I will be their God, and they shall be my people. And no longer shall each man teach his neighbor and each his brother, saying, 'Know the LORD,' for they shall all know me, from the least of them to the greatest, says the LORD; for I will forgive their iniquity, and I will remember their sin no more." (Jer. 31:31–34)

Twice during the celebration of the Passover psalms are sung from the group called *The Hallel* or *The Praise of God* (Pss. 113–118). The final hymn, known as *The Great Hallel,* is Psalm 136. It may have been this which they sang as "they went out to the Mount of Olives." (14:26)

The Night in the Garden: Praying and Watching (14:32–42)

The agony of Jesus depicted in this story is real. It is difficult to convey the intensity packed into the Greek words translated "greatly distressed and troubled." (Vs. 33) "Shuddering awe," "terrified surprise," "deep agitation" are some of the attempts which have been made to bring across the meaning.[31]

Jesus' prayer is one of intimate conversation and urgent petition. " 'Abba, Father, all things are possible to thee; remove this cup from me.' " (Vs. 36) This plea may represent a repetition (or continuation) of the temptation (1:12f.; cf. Matt. 4:1–11; Luke 4:1–13). Jesus may, in effect, be asking if he must go through with it *at all* or if he must go through with it *this way.* The cup which he asks to be removed is that cup of the covenant in his blood (vs. 24), i.e., his life! But again the temptation is resisted. His will is subjected to God's. " 'Yet not what I will, but what thou wilt.' " (Vs. 36) This has become the model prayer of his followers (cf. Matt. 6:10).

The disciples were asked to "watch" (vss. 32, 34, 37, 38). To "watch" means to wait for some person or some event believingly, trustingly, expectantly (cf. 13:32–37). This request recalled the vigil which God had commanded in commemoration of the deliverance of the people from bondage.

> It was a night of watching by the LORD, to bring them out of the land of Egypt; so this same night is a night of watching kept to the LORD by all the people of Israel throughout their generations. (Exod. 12:42)

But the disciples could not stay awake (cf. 13:32–37). Without comprehending his agony or participating in his prayer or sharing in his suffering they slept. And while they slept he was betrayed. Subsequent disciples in Mark's day throughout the Roman Empire would get his meaning *clearly.*

And is this not the way his disciples often fail him today—by sleeping? " 'Could you not watch one hour? Watch and pray that you may not enter into temptation; the spirit is indeed willing, but the flesh is weak.' " (Vss. 37f.)

The central significance of this whole story is Jesus' faithful acceptance of God's loving authority and his trustful obedience to God's purposeful will. Some New Testament scholars suggest that the use of this Aramaic word "Abba" (14:36) definitely goes back to Jesus himself, that it is an original and unique usage with him, and that it reflects Jesus' consciousness of, or at least an implicit claim to, a special and intimate relation to God.

Jesus Rejected and Crucified
Mark 14:53–65; 15:16–39

In this interpretive reflection we will center our attention upon Mark's accounts of the trial of Jesus before the Jewish authorities (14:53–65) and the crucifixion of Jesus by the Roman officials (15:16–39). It is crucial for our adequate understanding of these two events as Mark uses them in his Gospel to remember that his primary concern was not historical accuracy but rather evangelical affirmation of meaning and pastoral support for Christians caught in conflict. Also we must constantly keep in mind that these stories had been transmitted orally for a generation and shaped by the needs and practices of the early Christian community.

The Trial and Rejection (14:53–65)

Jesus is brought before a called meeting of the highest Jewish court, the Sanhedrin. Caiaphas the high priest presides (cf. Matt. 26:57). This body consisted of seventy-one members, including "the heads of the great priestly families" (Sadducees), scribes, and "lay elders" (Pharisees).[32] It is not certain whether the group before which Jesus was brought was an official and legal assembly or merely an informal gathering of some representatives of the three constituent groups (cf. vss. 53 and 55). (Mark's version of this event should be compared with the accounts in Matthew, Luke, and John.) It is obvious, however, that as Mark presents it, this was not a fair "trial." The council seeks "testimony against Jesus to put him to death," but they find none (vs. 55). The witnesses are false and conflict with one another (vss. 56, 59; cf. Deut. 19:15).

According to the second-century tractate *Sanhedrin* (a part of the Jewish legal tradition called *The Mishnah*), capital cases had to be decided "by a quorum of twenty-three judges."[33] Furthermore, the following regulations were to be observed:

The case must be begun with reasons for acquital and a conviction decided by a majority of at least two; the trial must be conducted in the daytime, but a verdict of conviction must not be reached until the following day. A trial, therefore, cannot be held on the eve of a Sabbath or a Festival-day.... Witnesses... must be admonished and warned against suppositions and mere hearsay.... For blasphemy the penalty is stoning, but the blasphemer is not culpable unless he pronounces the Name itself.[34]

It must be recognized that some (or all) of these rules of procedure may not have been developed by the end of the first quarter of the first century A.D. But it is also possible that the Sanhedrin did not even have the right to try capital cases at this time. Their only prerogative may have been to hold a "Grand Jury" hearing in order to prepare a brief to be submitted to the Roman procurator for formal and legal adjudication.

The charge which is specified against Jesus in Mark's account is that he had said he would " ' "destroy this temple that is made with hands, and in three days...build another, not made with hands." ' " (14:58; cf. 13:2; John 2:21f.) A statement such as this *might* have been falsely construed as blasphemy (cf. 2:7). The temple was understood to be the special dwelling place of God. The more probable meaning of this charge, however, is that Jesus had claimed he would dispose of the old system of religion and instigate a new order. This was what the Messiah would do. This seems to be what Mark was claiming had occurred in "the event of Jesus." The old Jewish liturgical cult and legal code had been abolished and a new mode of being in faithful obedience and responsible love had been inaugurated. The high priest presses Jesus on this point (vs. 60). Jesus remains silent (cf. Isa. 53:7). (You decide!) But the chief justice asks him again this time directly and explicitly: " 'Are you the Christ, the Son of the Blessed?' " (Vs. 61) (The phrase "the Blessed" is a reverential substitute for the word "God.") The question is illegal interrogation. It demands that the defendant convict himself. However, as Mark proclaims it, the time has come. Therefore, he portrays Jesus as replying unequivocally: " 'I am' " (cf. Matt. 26:64; Luke 22:70), and adding words which combine references to Daniel 7:13 and Psalm 110:1. (It is as if Mark is asking: "Can you believe it? A Messiah with no army or political organization at the mercy of his accusers?") At Jesus' reply Caiaphas cries "blasphemy."

It is very doubtful that even a direct claim to Messiahship could be legally equated with this religious crime. It is possible, however, that the definition of blasphemy was at this time elastic enough to be stetched to apply to Jesus' statement, particularly the reference to his enthronement at the right hand of God.[35] Also, as the story is preserved and presented, Jesus' acceptance of the title "Son of the Blessed" might have lent weight to the accusation. In any case the false charge sticks. The court is satisfied. Its purpose is accomplished. These people are looking for an excuse to get rid of this revolutionary trouble-maker. They think they have found one that will do. Therefore they all condemn him as "deserving death." (Vs. 64) By appropriating and employing this story in this form one question Mark may be asking is this: why and how do people try to get rid of him today?

Who is actually on trial here? Jesus, to be sure, but not Jesus alone. His accusers, the religious leaders, are also in the dock. And they are pronounced guilty. Furthermore, all Mark's readers are asked: "What do you think? How do you vote?" The implication is this: "By your verdict you in fact judge yourself."

Victory, Coronation, and Enthronement (15:16–39)

Mark intends to communicate profound meaning through his use of this symbolic account of the crucifixion. The language which is used and the way this narrative is constructed clearly indicate its purpose: to proclaim the Crucified as the Conqueror. Through the irony and the paradox the eyes of faith are able to read the positive word of God's victory in apparent defeat.

The victorious warrior is led by his military escort into "the place." (Vs. 16) The "whole battalion" is assembled for his coronation (vss. 16f.). The royal robe is draped upon his shoulders and the monarch's crown is fixed upon his head (vs. 17). The soldiers put a sceptor in his hand (Matt. 27:29) and kneel down "in homage to him." (Vs. 19) He is then taken and placed upon his throne (vss. 20–25) over which is placarded "The King of the Jews." (Vs. 26) There he reigns and there he dies. His crucifixion is his coronation!

The satanic forces of evil, bondage, and death had done their worst (cf. 15:33) and it appeared that they had won. But, on the contrary, in Jesus' humiliation, suffering, and death *they* had been defeated. Precisely because he would not save himself he saved others (vs. 31; cf. 10:45). Through his crucifixion Jesus firmly established the kingdom which he had preached and personified. The result is the immediate and present reign of God through his Son (vss. 37–39). Unwittingly the executioners of Jesus had declared his gospel. But their inscription over his throne must be modified. He is not just "The King of the Jews." He is the Ruler over *all*. For those who believe, this means forgiveness, freedom, and life. For those who follow him it will also mean his cross (8:34f.).

He Has Risen!
Mark 15:42—16:8

The burial of Jesus (15:42–47) is the solid affirmation of his death. Let there be no doubt about it. Jesus really died on the cross (vss. 44f.). In so doing he won the victory (15:16–39; 16:6f.). The resurrection of Jesus (16:1–8), as proclaimed by the evangelist Mark, is the sure confirmation of

Jesus' life which climaxed in his crucifixion. It is God's clear yes to his faithful Son (1:1; 14:61; 15:39). It is the ratification of Mark's Gospel. What he has been claiming about Jesus is true. He is indeed *Christus Victor.* The empty tomb is also God's declaration that Jesus is forever alive, authoritative, and active in the world (16:7f.), offering life to people and calling them to follow him.[36]

"He Has Risen . . . He Is Not Here . . . He Is Going Before You" (16:1-7)

Where *is* he? Certainly, as Mark tells the story, this was not the question in the minds of the women as they walked toward Joseph's "lovely garden" very early in the morning on the first day of the week. *They knew where he was.* He was in the place where dead people are naturally kept. He was in the grave. And they were going there to perform the final burial rites. They had bought spices and were bringing them to anoint his corpse (16:1).

The question which troubled Mary Magdalene, Mary the Mother of James, and Salome was simply, "'who will roll away the stone for us from the door of the tomb?'" (16:3) They were not wondering, "Where is he?" Not yet, anyway. As one would normally expect, they were seeking him among the dead. Through this opening scene of this brief one act resurrection drama Mark is perhaps asking his readers: Are we like these first Easter mourners? Are we looking for him in the sepulcher? Have we forgotten that he is not to be found among the dead but rather among the living?

At this point the original question becomes relevant. When the women enter the tomb and find the body of Jesus gone, they are frightened and struck with wonder (16:6). They would spontaneously think: "Where is he?" The address of the young man in white seems to anticipate this question: "'Do not be amazed; you seek Jesus of Nazareth, who was crucified. He has risen, he is not here; see the place where they laid him.'" (16:6)

Mark is saying: he is alive and active out there in the world, still working, teaching, healing, forgiving, liberating, and giving life to all who will hear and heed his call, "Come, follow me." He *cannot* be killed, or buried, or bound. He is present out there in the world wherever his action is occurring, in the way that he accomplishes the victory over the forces of sin, bondage, and death—the salvation of persons—through obedient self-giving love, through the cross.

Therefore, go! "'Go, tell his disciples and Peter that *he is going before you* [even as he did when he walked ahead of you on the road] to Galilee; there you will see him as he told you.'" (16:7, author's emphasis) Is it significant that it is Galilee, the place where it all started, the secular world, and *not* Jerusalem, the place where it ended, the sacred citadel, where Jesus will be met by his disciples? Do not look around here any longer. Go out there where he is, get with him, and follow him into life!

notes

PART I: METHODOLOGY

¹See, for example, Paul J. Achtemeier, *Mark: Proclamation Commentaries* (Philadelphia: Fortress Press, 1975), pp. v, 9f., 111–117; Willi Marxsen, *Mark the Evangelist: Studies on the Redaction History of the Gospel* (Nashville: Abingdon Press, 1969), Preface, p. 8; Etienne Trocmé, *The Formation of the Gospel According to Mark* (translated by Pamela Gaughan, Philadelphia: Westminster Press, 1975), pp. 1–86.

²While literary criticism remains an essential methodological step in adequately interpreting books within the New Testament, especially the Synoptic Gospels (Matthew, Mark, and Luke), and has gained renewed and increased significance in its recent expanded definition and expression (including the exploration of questions such as the relation of literary form to human meaning, structural form to material content, and the dynamic, creative character of language itself) its historical period of origin, refinement, and employment as a primary scholarly discipline can be dated roughly from the work of J. D. Michaelis, *Einleitung in die Göttlichen Schriften des Neuen Bundes (Introduction to The Holy Scriptures of the New Covenant),* 1750, to that of Burnett Hillman Streeter, *The Four Gospels,* published in London in 1924 (first edition). Also, it must be acknowledged that the current solution to the synoptic problem accepted by a majority of New Testament scholars (i.e., the priority of Mark, the existence of the hypothetical "Q" source, the use of Mark and "Q" by Matthew and Luke, plus special Matthew and special Luke material) has been challenged and debated since its initial proposal. Recently W. R. Farmer has contended for the answer to the literary relationships among the three Synoptic Gospels "first formulated by the eighteenth-century [German] scholar Johann Griesbach. This hypothesis maintains that Matthew was the earliest Gospel, that Luke used Matthew as a source, and that Mark used both." Joseph B. Tyson, *A Study of Early Christianity* (New York: Macmillan Publishing Company, Inc., 1973), p. 188. See William Reuben Farmer, *The Synoptic Problem* (New York: The Macmillan Company, 1964) and Tyson's discussion, op. cit., pp. 183–190.

³Two New Testament scholars who inaugurated and established this discipline of Gospel research were Martin Dibelius, *Die formgeschichte des Evangeliums (The Form Criticism of the Gospels),* in 1919, and Rudolf Bultmann, *Die Geschichte der synoptischen Tradition (The History of the Synoptic Tradition),* 1921. For the story of form criticism see Edgar V. McKnight, *What Is Form Criticism?* (Philadelphia: Fortress Press, 1969).

⁴For example: The controversy discourses (Mark 2:1–3:35), the parables (Mark 4:1–32), the miracles by the sea (Mark 4:35–5:43), the passion narrative (Mark 14:1–16:8). See Werner Georg Kümmel, *Introduction to the New Testament,* 14th Revised Edition, translated by A. J. Mattill, Jr., (Nashville: Abingdon Press, 1966), pp. 62f.

⁵Trocmé, *op. cit.*, pp. 215–259.

⁶Achtemeier, *op. cit.*, p. 111. Note the prominent role women play in Mark's Gospel (e.g., Mark 15:40–41, 47; 16:1–8).

⁷For a very informative treatment of this issue of history and/or faith in the Gospels see

the recent and helpful book by Norman Perrin, *Rediscovering the Teaching of Jesus* (New York: Harper and Row, 1967). For a clear and helpful introduction to the problem see Howard Clark Kee, Franklin W. Young, and Karlfried Froehlich, *Understanding the New Testament*, third edition (Englewood Cliffs, New Jersey: Prentice Hall, 1973), pp. 71–93. As has often been noted, the stated purpose of the Gospel of John is, to a great degree, the implicit purpose of the Gospels of Matthew, Mark, and Luke as well: "Now Jesus did many other signs in the presence of the disciples, which are not written in this book; but these are written that you may believe that Jesus is the Christ, the Son of God, and that believing you may have life in his name." (John 20:30–31)

⁸From this point onward authors, editors, and redactors of the final editions of the Gospels, those we read in the printed New Testament, i.e., the canonical texts, are synonymous. These designations may also be used for those who combined stages, or versions (parts) of individual Gospels before they were put into their final shape by the last redactor (author).

⁹For an excellent history and explanation of redaction criticism with helpful illustrations see Norman Perrin, *What Is Redaction Criticism?* (Philadelphia: Fortress Press, 1969).

¹⁰Achtemeier, *op. cit.*, p. 32.

¹¹For an explanation of the presuppositions, purposes, and methods of structual exegesis see Daniel Patte, *What Is Structural Exegesis?* (Philadelphia: Fortress Press, 1976).

PART II: ST. MARK SPEAKS

¹I have been encouraged in this precarious and audacious undertaking by some of my colleagues and students at Southwestern At Memphis, by some Methodist ministers with whom I discussed this idea at the 1977 Nashville Area Pastors' School held at Martin College, Pulaski, Tennessee, and by some writers and poets, mostly lay persons, at a conference on *Religion and Art* in Montreat, N.C., in August of 1977.

²Achtemeier, *Mark: Proclamation Commentaries* (Philadelphia: Fortress Press, 1975), p. 94. "Mark seems to go out of his way to portray some women as responding positively to Jesus (e.g., 5:28; 7:25; 14:3). In marked contrast to the twelve, the women who followed Jesus from Galilee to Jerusalem remained faithful to the end (contrast 15:40–47 with 14:50). It is they who alone are left to tend the buried corpse of Jesus (16:1), and they who are the first to learn of the empty tomb. In light of their faithfulness around the cross, it is highly unlikely that Mark intended the reader to think that as a result of their fearful reaction to such news (16:8) they disobeyed the angelic message to inform the disciples. There may be an intended note of irony here: the women must proclaim the good news of Jesus' resurrection to the disciples before the latter can embark on their own task of proclamation." See also *ibid.*, p. 111.

³See, for example, Vincent Taylor, *The Gospel According to St. Mark* (London: Macmillan and Co., Ltd., 1957), pp. 1–8; 26–31.

⁴In support of this view see, for example, Waldo Beach, *The Christian Life* (Richmond, Va.: CLC Press, 1966), pp. 124–129; Peter Berger, *A Rumour of Angels* (Garden City, N.Y.: Doubleday, 1969), pp. 69–72.

⁵The historical accuracy of the reference to Mark as "stump-fingered" in the *Anti-Marcionite Prologue to the Gospel of Mark* (second century A.D.) is at least questionable. Cf. Taylor, *op. cit.*, pp. 3f.

⁶Romans 1:7; 1 Corinthians 1:2; 2 Corinthians 1:1; Philippians 1:1.

⁷For further discussion of Mark's "universalism," see below. Also Achtemeier, *op. cit.*, pp. 23–38.

⁸Kümmel, *op. cit.*, p. 361.

⁹*The Oxford Annotated Bible with the Apocrypha, Revised Standard Version* (College Edition) (N.Y.: Oxford University Press, Inc., 1965), p. 1536. See also, Kümmel, *op. cit.,* p. 362. "The division of chapters which is usual today came into use soon after 1200. Tradition traces it back to Stephen Langton, archbishop of Canterbury (died 1228). Verse division derives from the Parisian book dealer, Robert Stephanus, and appeared for the first time in his edition of the New Testament in 1551."

¹⁰Achtemeier, *op. cit.,* p. 117.

¹¹*Ibid.,* p. 113.

¹²*Ibid.,* p. 112.

¹³Kümmel, *op. cit.,* p. 43. This is Kümmel's translation. He quotes the opening statement in the preceding paragraph in Greek. Some scholars, e.g., Kümmel (p. 43) suggest that only the first sentence in this quotation comes from "the presbyter John" and that the remainder of the quotation is Papias' own interpretation. This is possible but difficult to maintain on the basis of the Greek text of Eusebius alone. See also e.g., William L. Lane, *The Gospel According to Mark* in *The New International Commentary on the New Testament* series. (Grand Rapids, Michigan: William B. Eerdmans Publishing Company, 1974), p. 8.

¹⁴*Ibid.* This quotation from Kümmel includes a slight but important change. Kümmel (in the English) reads in the last part of this quote, "and what Aristion and the presbyter John, the Lord's *disciple,* were saying." (Italics added.) In the Greek text of Eusebius the word *disciple* is in the plural. The singular in Kümmel is confusing and perhaps misleading. The presbyter John is not to be identified with the Apostle John. The word "disciples" is being used here in the larger sense of "follower," not referring specifically to the "original twelve." But cf. further Kümmel, *Ibid.,* p. 172. According to Eusebius: "Yet Papias himself, according to the preface of his treatises, makes plain that he had in no way been a hearer and eyewitness of the sacred apostles, but teaches that he had received the articles of the faith from those who had known them, for he speaks as follows: 'And I shall not hesitate to append to the interpretations all that I ever learnt well from the presbyters and remember well, for of their truth I am confident. For unlike most I did not rejoice in them who say much, but in them who teach the truth, nor in them who recount the commandments of others, but in them who repeated those given to the faith by the Lord and derived from truth itself; but if ever anyone came who had followed the presbyters, I inquired into the words of the presbyters, what Andrew or Peter or Philip or Thomas or James or John or Matthew, or any other of the Lord's disciples, had said, and what Aristion and the presbyter John, the Lord's disciples, were saying. For I did not suppose that information from books would help me so much as the word of a living and surviving voice.' " Eusebius, *Ecclesiastical History,* III. XXXIX. 2–4. Translated by Kirsopp Lake, *The Loeb Classical Library, Eusebius,* (New York: G. P. Putnam's Sons, 1926), vol I, pp. 290–293.

¹⁵*Ibid.*

¹⁶Achtemeier, *op. cit.,* p. 112f.

¹⁷*Ibid.,* pp. 112. One current scholar, Etienne Trocmé, in a recent work, *The Formation of the Gospel According to Mark* (Philadelphia: Westminster Press, 1975) has suggested that we have three *main* "authors" of the Gospel according to Mark: one who is responsible for chapters 1–13; one who is responsible for chapters 14–16; and the final one who put the previous two together. This final editor-publisher was "an anonymous ecclesiastic of the Roman community." The date for the composition of "canonical Mark" is said to be between 65 and 85, probably during the decade 75–85 A.D. Trocmé, *ibid.,* pp. 215–248, esp. pp. 245–248. Trocmé argues the case for the following: Chapters 1–13: "The author to whom we propose attributing the original Mark could be Philip, the evangelizer of Samaria and the only one of the Seven, apart from Stephen, of whom we know a little, although the information we have about him is limited to what we find in one chapter of Acts (8) and a few verses in another (21.8ff.), if

we except the quite probable tradition that after the year 70 he lived at Hierapolis.... In short, Mark 1–13 must have been written in Palestine around the year 50 of our Christian era." *Ibid.,* pp. 257–259. Chapters 14–16: evolved in Jerusalem between the death of Jesus and the editorial combination of 1–13 and 14–16, rather earlier than later. "The Passion story which Mark used was the 'canonical' text that was read out at Jerusalem in the course of the liturgy which, on the occasion of the Jewish Passover, and perhaps also of other annual pilgrimages, commemorated the suffering, death, and resurrection of Jesus Christ; but it entered the Gospel in a slightly amplified Greek version, designed to establish the celebration of the feast in the non-Palestinian Churches." *Ibid.,* p. 62. A document "of a liturgical nature, which served perhaps for the annual commemoration of our Lord's Passion, came from Jerusalem and was attributed to Mark. Without having necessarily been its author, Mark may have translated, supplemented, and circulated it. From this small document, the name was transferred to the canonical Mark, thus placing it under quasi-apostolic patronage and giving it indirectly a share in the reflected authority of Peter, with whom tradition associated John Mark of Jerusalem. The name of the editor who combined this 'Passion according to Saint Mark' with Mark 1–13 will never be known." *Ibid.,* pp. 246–248.

[18]*Enthusiasm.* Gr. *enthousiasmos,* fr. *enthousiazein* to be inspired or possessed by the god, fr. *entheos, enthous* inspired. *Webster's New Collegiate Dictionary* (C. and G. Merriam Co., Springfield, Mass., 1951), p. 275.

[19]Achtemeier, *op. cit.,* pp. 77f. See also pp. 87, 99, 101, 107.

[20]See, e.g., Kümmel, *op. cit.,* pp. 71f. Cf. also Achtemeier, *op. cit.,* p. 81.

[21]Kümmel, *op. cit.,* pp. 71f. Achtemeier, *op. cit.,* p. 91.

[22]See, for example, the following: John S. Dunne, *A Search for God in Time and Memory* (N.Y.: Macmillan, 1969); Richard R. Niebuhr, *Experiential Religion* (N.Y.: Harper & Row, 1972); T. Stoneburner, ed., *Parable, Myth and Language;* Sallie McFague TeSelle, *Speaking in Parables: A Study in Metaphor and Theology* (Philadelphia: Fortress, 1975); Brian Wicker, *The Story-Shaped World: Fiction and Metaphysics* (Notre Dame, Ind.: University of Notre Dame Press, 1975); James B. Wiggins, ed., *Religion as Story* (N.Y.: Harper & Row, 1975); James McClendon, *Biography as Theology* (Nashville: Abingdon, 1974).

[23]"The Hellenistic world into which the Christian faith moved within the first decade or two of its life, while producing a variety of kinds of literature, religious and secular, offered a similar paucity of models for our canonical Gospels. A form of literature called the 'novel' or 'romance' was in its formative stages about this time, a form which bears some resemblance in type and structure to our Gospels, but it flowered as a form only after the canonical Gospels had already been written, and had much greater influence on the later, non-canonical acts of the various apostles, such as the Acts of Paul and Thecla, the Acts of Thomas, the Acts of Peter, and many others. From a literary point of view, our Gospels belong as much to the formative stage of this literary type as they do to a genre which was established before the Gospels were written.

"There was, in short, no set kind of literary form to which the author of the first Gospel could turn, as did Paul and others when they made use of the form of the epistle." Achtemeier, *op. cit.,* p. 5. See also, e.g., Howard Clark Kee, *Community of the New Age: Studies in Mark's Gospel* (Philadelphia: Westminster Press, 1977), p. 16.

[24]Although I do not claim specific documentary or scholarly support for these Markan motives, on the basis of our general knowledge of the world-views, folkways, and cultural expressions of the Roman Empire of the first century, East and West, and our growing knowledge of the history of the early church, I believe them to be logical and likely. I do not intend to imply in the discussion which follows that "the historical Mark" had *necessarily* read or that he even knew of any of Paul's letters. See also the discussion of "Why, then, a gospel?" in Achtemeier, *op. cit.,* pp. 5–7.

[25] In the ancient world when a person consciously claimed to be speaking for the god he or she usually said so; for example, the priestesses and priests of the oracle at Delphi in Greece (first on behalf of the great Mother Earth goddess, then later on behalf of Appollo); the Hebrew prophets of Yahweh within Israel (in the OT) and the Apostle Paul (e.g., 1 Cor. 2:1–3:23, esp. 2:1, 7, 10, 13). Of course, an argument from silence is not conclusive. However, on the basis of the current widely accepted results of literary criticism, form criticism, and redaction criticism, I believe it is logical and likely that Mark would say something very much like what I have put in his mouth here.

[26] See pp. 95–97.

[27] Achtemeier, *op. cit.*, p. 117. Howard Clark Kee, makes a strong and impressive case for a provenance (original setting) for the Gospel of Mark, as we now have it, in a radical rural eschatological community of Hellenistic (Greek-speaking) Jewish Christians, composed, among others, of itinerant charismatic preachers, prophets, exorcists, and healers located in Syria. This community suffered the persecutions, trials, and tribulations which other Jews suffered during the Jewish rebellion which, though centered in Jerusalem-Palestine, spread widely in the Eastern portion of the Roman Empire. Howard Clark Kee. *Community of the New Age* (Philadelphia: Westminster Press, 1977, p. 105).

[28] This expectation was voiced in the Old Testament especially by psalmists (e.g., Pss. 2, 18, 20, 21, 45, 72, 101, 110, 132) and prophets (e.g., Isa. 9:2–7; 11:1–9; 32:1ff.; Jer. 33:14ff.; Ezek. 34:23; 43:1–10; Zech. 8:1–13; Mal. chaps. 3–4) and in the intertestamental period (between the book of Daniel, ca. 165 B.C. and the life of Jesus) by Zealots, Pharisees, and other groups.

[29] For a summary chronological analysis of Mark 11–16 see Achtemeier, *op. cit.*, pp. 84f.

[30] Kee, *op. cit.*, p. 46.

[31] *Ibid.*, p. 110f.

[32] Achtemeier, *op. cit.*, p. 34.

[33] *Ibid.*, p. 35.

[34] Kee, *op. cit.*, p. 121f.

[35] Achtemeier, *op. cit.*, p. 34.

[36] *Ibid.*

[37] *Ibid.*, p. 45.

[38] *Ibid.*, p. 42.

[39] *Ibid.*, pp. 45–47.

[40] *Ibid.*, pp. 102–110.

[41] *Ibid.*, pp. 106–107.

[42] *Ibid.*, p. 107.

[43] *Ibid.*, p. 108.

[44] *Ibid.*, pp. 109f.

[45] Kee *op. cit.*, pp. 77–105.

[46] Jacob Brubaker Smith, *Greek-English Concordance to the New Testament.* (Scottdale, Pennsylvania: Herald Press, 1955), p. 157.

[47] Kee, *op. cit.*, p. 51.

[48] *Ibid.*, p. 52.

⁴⁹*Ibid.*

⁵⁰*Ibid.*, p. 53.

⁵¹William Wrede. *Das Messiasgeheimnis in den Evangelien.* (Göttingen: Vandenhoeck P. Ruprecht 1901; 2nd ed., 1913).

⁵²See above in the section "Titles for Jesus Are Telling."

⁵³Kee, *op. cit.*, pp. 53f.

⁵⁴E.g., 1:14, 16, 21; 2:1; 3:7 (?), 13 (?); 4:1 (?); 5:1, 20, 21 (?); 6:1 (?), *45, 53; 7:24, *31; 8:10, 22, *27; 9:30, 33; 10:1 (the "region of Judea and beyond the Jordan"), 32 ("on the road, going up to Jerusalem"), 46 (Jericho); 11:1 ("near to Jerusalem," to Bethphage and Bethany, at the Mount of Olives), 11 ("And he entered Jerusalem, and went into the temple; and when he had looked around at everything, as it was already late, he went out to Bethany with the twelve."), 12, 15 (Jerusalem), 27 (Jerusalem); 14:3 (Bethany), 17 (Jerusalem), 32.

⁵⁵Achtemeier, *op. cit.*, p. 13.

⁵⁶From Kee, *op. cit.*, pp. 62f. See Taylor, *op. cit.*, pp. 107–111.

⁵⁷From the New Testament: An Introduction by Norman Perrin, © 1974 by Harcourt Brace Jovanovich, Inc. Reprinted by permission of the publishers.

PART III: ST. MARK HEARD

¹William Barclay, *The Gospel of Mark: The Daily Study Bible* (Edinburgh: The Saint Andrew Press, 1958), p. 50.

²Paul S. Minear, *The Gospel According to Mark: The Layman's Bible Commentary, Vol. 17* (Richmond, Virginia: John Knox Press, 1962), p. 60.

³Warren N. Quanbeck in *The Oxford Annotated Bible, College Edition* (New York: Oxford University Press, 1962), p. 1472.

⁴Minear, *op. cit.*, p. 18.

⁵Paul J. Achtemeier, *Mark: Proclamation Commentaries* (Philadelphia: Fortress Press, 1975), pp. 23, 25, 24–25.

⁶Minear, *op. cit.*, p. 12.

⁷*Ibid.*, p. 16.

⁸Tacitus, *Annals XV. 44.* In Charles Kingsley Barrett, *The New Testament Background: Selected Documents* (N.Y.: Harper & Brothers, 1961), pp. 15–16.

⁹Achtemeier, *op. cit.*, p. 115.

¹⁰Vincent Taylor, *The Gospel According to St. Mark* (London: Macmillan and Co., Ltd., 1952), p. 152.

¹¹*Ibid.*

¹²*Ibid.*

¹³Frederick C. Grant in "The Introduction to Mark" in *The Interpreters Bible, Vol. 7* (New York: Abingdon - Cokesbury Press, 1951), p. 643.

¹⁴*Ibid.*

¹⁵Taylor, *op. cit.*, p. 161. Quoted from B. Hag. 15a.

¹⁶*Ibid.*, p. 162.

[17] See Minear, *op. cit.*, pp. 53f.

[18] *Ibid.*, pp. 56–57.

[19] *Ibid.*, p. 58.

[20] Günther Bornkamm, *Jesus of Nazareth* (N.Y.: Harper & Row Publishers, 1960), p. 72.

[21] Minear, *op. cit.*, p. 79.

[22] *Ibid.*, p. 85.

[23] Taylor, *op. cit.*, p. 381.

[24] Minear, *op. cit.*, p. 103.

[25] *Ibid.*

[26] Taylor, *op. cit.*, p. 433.

[27] *Ibid.*, p. 470.

[28] Minear, *op. cit.*, p. 112.

[29] For discussion of the question see Taylor, *op. cit.*, pp. 664–667.

[30] *Ibid.*, p. 544.

[31] *Ibid.*, p. 552.

[32] *Ibid.*, p. 565.

[33] *Ibid.*, p. 645.

[34] *Ibid.*

[35] *Ibid.*, pp. 569f.

[36] In this final "interpretive reflection" on the resurrection of Jesus I have chosen not to enter into a discussion of the historical questions and literary problems, but rather simply to communicate my understanding of the essential elements of Mark's "Easter message." For a recent brief, readable, and helpful critical study of the resurrection as it is proclaimed in the Synoptic Gospels see Norman Perrin, *The Resurrection According to Matthew, Mark, and Luke* (Philadelphia: Fortress Press, 1977).

index to references in Mark

1:1, 32, 39, 42, 48, 50, 54, 55, 66, 71, 92, 96, 98, 135
1:1-3, 40, 71
1:1-13, 71, 72, 73
1:1-15, 69
1:1-20, 98-104
1:2, 101
1:2-3, 99
1:2-8, 98, 99
1:2-15, 99
1:3, 52, 53, 63, 101
1:4, 45, 101
1:4-8, 99, 101
1:4-15, 99
1:5, 101
1:5-6, 101
1:6-8, 16
1:7, 65, 101
1:7-8, 101
1:9, 16, 49, 128
1:9-11, 40, 43, 55, 57
1:9-13, 98, 102-103
1:10, 16, 63
1:10-11, 16, 71
1:11, 16, 32, 42, 43, 44, 48, 65, 101
1:12, 63, 77, 103, 131
1:12-13, 44
1:13, 46
1:14, 32, 39, 44, 45, 57, 71, 98
1:14—3:6, 72
1:14-15, 16, 69, 73, 98, 103
1:14—8:26, 71, 72
1:15, 50, 51, 57, 76, 82, 100, 104, 105, 108
1:16-20, 39, 81, 98, 104-105
1:16—3:6, 73
1:17, 65
1:18, 63, 104
1:20, 32, 63, 104
1:21, 63, 67
1:21-22, 67
1:21-28, 54, 67, 77, 104, 105-106, 112
1:21-45, 105-107
1:21—2:12, 57
1:22, 76, 83, 102, 106
1:23, 44, 65
1:23-28, 102, 108
1:24, 40, 48, 49, 57, 105
1:25, 76
1:26, 105
1:27, 18, 105
1:28, 63, 65
1:29, 63
1:29-31, 106
1:29-45, 104, 106-107
1:30, 63
1:31, 63
1:32-34, 69
1:34, 57, 65, 76, 106
1:35, 72
1:35-39, 106
1:38, 100
1:39, 69
1:40, 17, 107
1:40-45, 107
1:41, 18, 107
1:42, 63, 107
1:43, 63, 65, 123
1:44, 107
1:45, 69
1—5, 16

2:1, 82
2:1-2, 69
2:1-5, 17
2:1-12, 17, 56, 57, 65, 82, 91, 108
2:1—3:6, 88, 104, 107-110
2:2, 39, 63, 82, 108, 109, 110
2:3-5, 108
2:5, 18, 82, 108, 109
2:6, 40, 82, 109, 110
2:7, 44, 133
2:8, 63
2:8-11, 82
2:9, 108
2:9-11, 109
2:10, 65, 66, 82
2:11, 18, 108
2:12, 18, 63, 109
2:13, 67, 69, 72
2:13-17, 82, 83, 108
2:13—3:6, 67, 76
2:15, 69, 72, 83, 85
2:15-17, 40, 108, 109
2:16, 44, 85, 110
2:17, 108
2:18, 110
2:18-20, 83, 108
2:18-22, 40, 82
2:18-28, 77
2:19, 108
2:20, 40, 45, 65
2:21, 108
2:23, 69, 72
2:23-27, 86
2:23-28, 17, 18, 108
2:23—3:6, 39, 40, 45, 57, 82
2:24, 110
2:27, 63, 66, 86, 108
2:27-28, 56, 86
2:28, 52, 53, 65

3:1, 72
3:1-2, 18
3:1-4, 17, 18
3:1-6, 17, 65, 77, 86, 108
3:4, 86, 108
3:4-6, 87
3:5, 18
3:6, 18, 32, 45, 57, 63, 110
3:7, 72, 111
3:7-10, 111
3:7-12, 55, 69, 73
3:7-31, 67
3:7-35, 110-113
3:7—6:13, 72
3:11, 42, 48, 65, 71, 101, 110, 111, 112-113
3:12, 123
3:13, 63, 72
3:13-15, 32, 64, 70, 71, 118
3:13—6:6, 73
3:14, 69, 118
3:15, 72, 118
3:19, 72
3:19-21, 61
3:19-27, 76
3:20-28, 66
3:20-35, 71
3:21, 45, 111
3:21-29, 40, 111
3:22, 45, 111, 112
3:22-27, 102, 104, 111-112
3:23, 63, 69, 72
3:23-27, 53, 57
3:24-26, 112
3:27, 57, 112
3:28-30, 57, 112
3:29, 112
3:29-30, 112
3:30, 112
3:31, 111
3:31-35, 16, 39, 111
3:33-35, 69
3:34-35, 33, 100
3:35, 42
4:1, 67, 69, 111
4:1-9, 53, 67
4:1-34, 113-114
4:1-41, 67
4:2, 63
4:2-9, 113
4:5, 63
4:10, 64
4:10-34, 71
4:11, 63
4:13, 63
4:14-19, 113
4:14-20, 113

4:15, 63
4:16, 63
4:17, 39, 40, 45, 63
4:19, 60
4:20, 60
4:21, 63
4:21-23, 114
4:21-25, 108
4:22, 114
4:23, 114
4:24, 63, 114
4:25, 114
4:26, 50
4:26-29, 53, 61, 108, 113, 114-115
4:29, 63
4:30, 50
4:30-32, 53, 113
4:30-34, 115
4:32-34, 69
4:33, 67
4:33-34, 47, 69
4:34, 64
4:35, 63
4:35-41, 17, 54, 76, 80, 115, 116-117
4:35—6:6, 115-118
4:38, 53, 67, 116
4:39, 116
4:40, 116
4:41, 18, 116

5:1-13, 17, 55
5:1-20, 65, 115, 117
5:1-43, 67
5:2, 63
5:7, 42, 48, 71, 101
5:12, 89
5:13, 63
5:17, 69
5:19, 52, 53
5:19-20, 65, 66
5:20, 69
5:21-24, 17, 116, 118
5:24-34, 65
5:25, 117
5:25-34, 116, 117
5:28, 117
5:29, 63
5:30, 63
5:34, 73, 117
5:35, 67
5:35-43, 17, 57, 116, 118
5:36, 63
5:41, 18
5:42, 63
5:43, 65, 123

6:1, 65, 67, 72
6:1-6, 67, 116, 118
6:2, 69, 118
6:4, 51, 63
6:6, 65, 69, 73
6:7, 63, 69, 83, 119
6:7-12, 61
6:7-13, 32, 64, 65, 70, 71, 77, 118
6:7-56, 118-120
6:7—8:21, 73
6:8, 119
6:10, 63, 119
6:12, 70, 119
6:12-13, 69
6:13, 69
6:14-29, 40, 45, 95, 118, 120
6:14-56, 120
6:14—8:26, 73
6:15, 51
6:25, 63
6:27, 63
6:30, 70, 71, 72
6:30-44, 57, 65, 67, 91, 118, 121
6:31, 63, 64
6:34, 40, 45, 67, 69, 80
6:35-44, 120
6:45, 63
6:45-50, 76
6:45-52, 118, 120
6:45-53, 72
6:47, 72
6:50, 63
6:52, 120
6:53-56, 111, 118
6:54, 63
6:54-56, 69
6:55, 69
6:56, 65, 69

7:1-8, 39, 120, 121
7:1-15, 120
7:1-23, 18, 67, 77, 83, 84, 88, 121
7:1—8:26, 120-122
7:3, 120, 121
7:4, 121
7:5, 106, 121
7:5-13, 57
7:6-8, 83
7:8, 106, 121, 122
7:9, 63, 121
7:9-13, 120, 121-122
7:10, 122
7:13, 121
7:14, 63, 72

7:14-23, 39, 120, 122
7:16—8:26, 120
7:18, 63
7:19, 120, 122
7:20-23, 122
7:24-30, 61, 65, 121
7:24-37, 28
7:24—8:10, 120, 121
7:28, 52, 53
7:31, 72
7:31-37, 57, 61, 121
7:33, 64
7:35, 63
7:36, 65

8:1, 63
8:1-10, 57, 65, 121
8:10, 63
8:11, 67, 69
8:11-13, 120
8:11-21, 67
8:13, 76
8:14-21, 120
8:21, 63
8:21-26, 69
8:22-26, 61, 73, 120
8:22-30, 92
8:26, 65, 71
8:27, 28, 71
8:27-30, 122, 123-124
8:27-33, 40, 46
8:27-37, 122-125
8:27—9:1, 33
8:27—9:50, 72
8:27—10:45, 73
8:27—10:52, 73
8:28, 51, 123
8:29, 50, 71, 123
8:29-31, 56
8:30, 65, 123
8:30-31, 50
8:31, 32, 33, 34, 46, 47, 48, 54, 67, 69, 70, 97, 123, 124
8:31-32, 46
8:31-33, 46, 57, 122, 124
8:31-37, 81
8:31-38, 77
8:31—9:1, 32, 40
8:31—9:50, 67
8:32, 47, 69
8:32-33, 48
8:33, 48, 124
8:34, 47, 63, 67, 80, 124, 134
8:34-37, 122, 124-125
8:34-38, 33, 49, 76
8:34—9:1, 33, 40, 47, 54, 64, 70, 88, 95
8:35, 27
8:38, 56, 97
8:38—9:1, 80, 96
8—10, 48

9, 16
9:1, 32, 50, 59, 63, 80, 104
9:2, 64
9:2-8, 34, 40, 47, 49, 71
9:2-13, 32, 33, 55
9:7, 42, 48, 101
9:9, 32, 34, 56, 65
9:9-13, 34
9:9-14, 40
9:11-13, 43
9:12, 34, 48
9:14-27, 54
9:15, 63
9:17, 53, 67
9:20, 63
9:24, 63

9:28, 64
9:30-32, 32, 40, 46, 47, 48, 57
9:31, 32, 34, 47, 54, 63, 67, 69
9:33-34, 46, 47, 49
9:33-37, 71
9:35, 57
9:35-37, 47, 49
9:38, 53, 67
9:38-39, 70
9:38-40, 97
9:38-41, 49, 71
9:38-50, 88
9:41, 50
9:42, 93
9:42-50, 71
9:49, 40, 61

10, 125-127
10:1, 40, 67, 69, 72, 76, 111, 125
10:1-45, 67
10:2-12, 125
10:11, 63
10:13-16, 125
10:14, 125
10:15, 33, 50, 125, 126
10:17, 53, 67, 72, 125
10:17-22, 54, 81, 125-126
10:17-31, 33
10:18, 69, 125
10:20, 125
10:20-25, 71
10:21, 80, 125
10:22, 126
10:23, 50, 125
10:23-25, 126
10:23-31, 126-127
10:25, 27, 126
10:26, 125, 126
10:27, 125, 126
10:28, 125, 126
10:28-31, 39, 40, 76, 95
10:29, 57
10:29-31, 32, 39, 50, 95, 126
10:30, 125, 126, 127
10:31, 125, 127
10:32, 69, 72
10:32-34, 32, 40, 57, 125
10:33-34, 46, 47, 48
10:34-45, 77
10:35, 53, 67
10:35-41, 46, 47, 49
10:35-45, 32, 33, 40, 77, 88, 125
10:37-39, 134
10:38-45, 47, 88
10:41, 69
10:42, 63
10:42-45, 47, 49, 125
10:43, 33, 93
10:45, 32, 56, 57, 77, 103, 134
10:46, 72
10:46-51, 17
10:46-52, 49, 54, 67, 91, 125
10:47, 51, 68, 69
10:48, 51, 68
10:51, 53
10:52, 63

11, 127
11:1, 41, 72
11:1-10, 40, 65, 66, 91, 127
11:1-11, 51, 59
11:1—12:44, 73
11:1—13:37, 73
11:2, 63
11:3, 52, 53, 63
11:9, 52

11:10, 50, 68
11:11, 41
11:11-12, 72
11:11—16:8, 72
11:12, 41
11:12-14, 16
11:12-25, 28, 92, 93
11:12-33, 67
11:15, 69
11:15-19, 16, 54, 77, 127
11:17, 63, 65, 67
11:19, 72
11:20, 16, 41
11:21, 53, 67
11:27, 41
11:27-33, 127-128
11:27—12:40, 83
11:28, 127
11:29-33, 127
11:31, 128
11:33, 127, 128
11—12, 127-129
11—16, 41, 70, 95

12, 57, 127
12:1, 41, 69
12:1-5, 16
12:1-8, 16
12:1-11, 16, 67, 127, 128
12:1-12, 16, 40, 57
12:6, 42, 48
12:6-8, 16
12:9, 16, 52, 53
12:10, 16
12:10-11, 16
12:11, 52
12:13, 40, 41, 67
12:13-16, 17
12:13-17, 17, 88, 127, 128-129
12:13-34, 67
12:13-37, 54
12:13-44, 67
12:14, 53
12:17, 17, 95, 127
12:18, 41, 67
12:19, 53
12:25, 71
12:28-33, 87
12:28-34, 33, 39, 57, 80, 81, 127, 129
12:29, 52
12:29-31, 87
12:30, 52
12:31, 87
12:32, 53
12:34, 50
12:35, 41, 67
12:35-37, 50
12:36, 52
12:37, 52, 53
12:38, 67
12:43, 63

13, 33, 40, 54, 58, 59, 60, 70, 76, 77, 80, 88, 95, 104, 129
13:1, 41, 53, 67
13:1-5, 58, 69, 73
13:1-32, 67
13:2, 133
13:3, 41, 64
13:4, 58
13:5, 58, 59, 69
13:5-31, 58
13:5-37, 73
13:6, 58, 65
13:7, 58, 59
13:7-8, 38, 94

13:8, 58, 59
13:8-13, 59
13:9, 58, 59
13:9-13, 32, 40, 71, 80, 95
13:9-27, 94
13:10, 28, 32, 59
13:11, 32, 58
13:12, 58, 80
13:12-13, 39
13:13, 59, 60
13:14, 38
13:14-23, 71
13:14-30, 58
13:20, 32, 52, 53
13:21, 65
13:21-22, 50, 58
13:21-23, 58, 59
13:23, 32, 59
13:24-25, 60
13:24-26, 59
13:25, 80
13:26, 32, 56, 96, 97
13:27, 59
13:28-31, 58
13:29-31, 32
13:30, 59, 80
13:31, 102
13:32-37, 33, 55, 58, 59, 131
13:33, 59
13:35-37, 59
13:37, 60, 73

14, 41
14:1, 41
14:1-2, 40
14:1-12, 73
14:1—16:8, 73, 129
14:3, 72
14:3-9, 40, 41, 47
14:8, 41
14:9, 29, 32
14:10-11, 41
14:10—15:47, 40
14:12, 41
14:12-14, 129
14:12-25, 41, 67
14:12-41, 33
14:13, 54
14:13—16:8, 73
14:14, 53
14:17-21, 41
14:17-25, 32
14:17—15:39, 95
14:19, 69
14:21, 48, 56
14:22, 130
14:22-25, 16
14:22-26, 129-131
14:24, 131
14:25, 32, 59, 104
14:26, 131
14:26-31, 41
14:27, 45, 48
14:27-31, 47
14:28, 32, 34, 47
14:32, 131
14:32-41, 130
14:32-42, 32, 41, 47, 129, 131
14:32-50, 77
14:33, 69, 131
14:34, 63, 131
14:36, 96, 100, 131, 132
14:37, 131, 132
14:37-38, 33
14:38, 131
14:41, 56
14:41-42, 41

14:43, 63
14:43-50, 41
14:43—15:39, 57, 82
14:45, 63
14:47, 47
14:49, 48, 65, 67
14:49-50, 47
14:50, 47, 71
14:51-52, 31, 61
14:53, 132
14:53-65, 41, 55, 132-134
14:53-72, 95
14:53—15:32, 76
14:53—15:39, 77
14:53—16:8, 71
14:55, 132
14:56, 132
14:58, 133
14:59, 132
14:60, 133
14:60-72, 47
14:61, 42, 50, 70, 71, 92, 101, 133, 135
14:61-62, 56
14:62, 56, 60, 65, 66
14:64, 52, 134
14:65, 69
14:66-72, 41
14:71, 69, 95
14—16, 41, 48, 59, 130

15, 41, 42, 48, 92
15:1, 41, 63
15:1-5, 41
15:1-15, 95
15:1-39, 33
15:2, 50
15:6-15, 41
15:8, 69
15:9, 50
15:12, 50
15:16, 41, 134
15:16-20, 41
15:16-39, 32, 128, 132, 134
15:17, 134
15:18, 50, 69
15:19, 134
15:20-25, 134
15:21-41, 41
15:25-26, 50
15:26, 134
15:29, 29
15:31, 134
15:32, 50
15:33, 41, 117, 134
15:33-39, 55
15:34, 41
15:39, 40, 42, 46, 48, 71, 92, 96, 101, 135
15:40, 47
15:42, 41
15:42-47, 41, 134
15:42—16:8, 134-135
15:43, 50
15:44, 134

16, 42, 48, 58
16:1, 47, 135
16:1-7, 135
16:3, 135
16:1-8, 32, 47, 55, 57, 71, 76, 77, 134
16:6, 34, 134, 135
16:6-8, 34
16:7, 32, 47, 135
16:8, 59

LIBRARY OF DAVIDSON COLLEGE